REMEMBERING
GROTON

REMEMBERING

GROTON

tales from

EAST OF THE THAMES

Carol W. Kimball

THE History PRESS

Published by The History Press
Charleston, SC 29403
www.historypress.net

All images are from the author's collection unless otherwise noted.

First published 2008

Manufactured in the United States

ISBN 978.1.59629.513.1

Library of Congress Cataloging-in-Publication Data

Kimball, Carol W.
Groton : tales from east of the Thames / Carol W. Kimball.
p. cm.
ISBN 978-1-59629-513-1
1. Groton (Conn. : Town)--History--Anecdotes. 2. Groton (Conn. : Town)--Social life and customs--Anecdotes. 3. Groton (Conn. : Town)--Biography--Anecdotes. 4. Groton (Conn. : Town)--History, Naval--Anecdotes. I. Title.
F104.G84K526 2008
974.6'5--dc22
2008025946

Notice: The information in this book is true and complete to the best of our knowledge. It is offered without guarantee on the part of the author or The History Press. The author and The History Press disclaim all liability in connection with the use of this book.

CONTENTS

ACKNOWLEDGEMENTS

The columns reproduced in this book, unless otherwise noted, appeared first in *The Day*, a newspaper published in New London, Connecticut. I am grateful for permission to use this material.

I also wish to express thanks to Jim Streeter for his help with illustrative material and to Rachael and Christine McGuire for their expert technical assistance.

INTRODUCTION

Groton, incorporated from New London in 1705, lies in southeastern Connecticut, bounded by the Thames River at the west, the Mystic River at the east and Long Island Sound at the south. Within its more than forty-five square miles are a number of villages, fire districts and political subdivisions, all of which occupy a distinct part of the town. Each has made its own contribution to Groton's history.

These communities include the City of Groton, once called Groton Bank; the central, level section called Poquonnock or Poquonnock Bridge; Noank; West Mystic; Center Groton; Pleasant Valley; and the Naval Submarine Base. Sections of the communities of Mystic and Old Mystic lying west of the Mystic River are also part of the town of Groton, adding variety to the picture.

Groton, with its wide array of population centers, has produced a rich tapestry of history. Some of these tales are recorded in this volume.

THE BEGINNINGS

JOHN WINTHROP THE FOUNDER

The town of Groton celebrated its 300th anniversary in 2005, turning its attention to the founder, John Winthrop Jr., who had so much influence on the area's early years.

Winthrop was the eldest son of Governor John Winthrop, the man who led the settlement of the Massachusetts Bay Colony. Winthrop Jr. inherited his father's executive abilities. The younger Winthrop did not come to Boston in 1630 with the main body of settlers; he remained behind in England, managing the family estate in Suffolk and acting as business manager for the new colony. This Suffolk manor, by the way, was named Groton.

Winthrop Jr. finally sailed for the New World in 1631, bringing with him an extensive library and barrels of scientific equipment, as well as seeds of medicinal plants and herbs. He was known as a physician, dabbled in metaphysics and was eager to explore mineral deposits in the new land. Early on, he obtained a monopoly for the manufacture of iron and searched in vain for deposits of iron ore.

In the late fall of 1645, he was sent to explore the territory that is now southeastern Connecticut, discovered years earlier during the Pequot War. He chose a spot for a new colony at the mouth of the Thames River and in the spring began the settlement of Pequot Plantation, later New London. The original colony stretched eastward to the Mystic River and northward to include present-day Ledyard and Montville.

Winthrop crossed the Thames and wandered through the plains of Poquonnock, where he found land to his liking. Poquonnock, an Algonkian word, means "cleared land" where natives had prepared ground to plant crops. Winthrop envisioned a manor farm, like his Groton estate in England, run by tenant farmers. Soon after Pequot Plantation was established, the town granted him a large portion of that level land, including today's Bluff Point, Groton Long Point and Mumford Cove.

Winthrop obtained this property but never lived there. He had trouble establishing a manor farm. Tenant farmers were scarce in an environment where every man could own land and be his own boss.

John Winthrop Jr., founder of Pequot Plantation and later governor of Connecticut for eighteen years.

Winthrop served eighteen years as governor of Connecticut, renting the farm to various parties. After the governor's death in 1676, his son, Fitz-John Winthrop, continued to lease the property. A later tenant was Thomas Mumford, for whom the adjacent cove is named.

There is no evidence that Winthrop called this farm Groton. He referred to it simply as his "Great Farm." However, it became the custom to use the name Groton for land east of the Thames. The earliest example is found in the Winthrop papers, in a letter written by John Plumbe in October 1665 describing the appearance of a meteor he saw, "I being then rowing my boat to Groton." But, however it happened, when the east side of the colony became an independent town in 1705, the name chosen was Groton in honor of Winthrop, its leading citizen.

Written for the Groton Tercentennial Committee.

GROTON'S OLD RED HOUSE

The Hive of the Averys

The old red house known as the Hive of the Averys, a legendary landmark in Groton, stood for more than two centuries on land that is now southwest of the junction of Poquonnock Road and the Long Hill Road. So many Averys lived in this house that it was nicknamed "the Hive."

The first James Avery came to New London about 1651 and moved to Poquonnock after 1657. He built his house somewhere between Great Brook and the foot of Fort Hill, north of present Route 1. When his oldest son, James Avery Jr., married Debora Stallion in January 1670 or '71, the bride's father, mariner Edward Stallion, gave the couple a farm on Birch Plain "with the house, barn, fences and all other privileges and appurtenances."

The house, which became known as the Avery homestead, was probably a simple cottage in the beginning, but over the years many additions were made. In 1684, James Jr. bought the old Blinman church in New London for six pounds, promising to remove the aged structure within a month. According to tradition, he recycled the lumber and built a wing on the west side of his residence.

By 1890, a sprawling, picturesque dwelling had evolved. A familiar sight to Groton residents, it was a unique structure with great chimneys, angles and gables and an unusual second-story overhang. A small lean-to was tacked onto the northern end.

Groton's famous Hive of the Averys as it appeared before its destruction by fire on July 20, 1894.

The first railroad bridge built across the Thames River in 1889 posed a threat to the old homestead. New tracks were laid from Poquonnock to connect with the bridge. Original plans had tracks passing right through the house, but adjustments were made and the overpass and tracks were relocated. However, tracks still passed within a few yards of the western gable.

Through the years, numerous Avery descendants occupied the old red house. The last owner, James Denison Avery, was elected town clerk of Groton in 1874. As was the custom, he kept all the town records in his home. All town business was transacted there, for there was no town hall.

Shortly after 10:00 p.m. on Friday, July 20, 1894, an overnight guest in the Hive discovered that the old house was on fire. She gave the alarm, but flames had made such headway that Avery and his family and guests barely escaped in their nightclothes. There was no fire department. In minutes the old structure was reduced to ashes. Only the two chimneys and heaps of charred timbers remained.

The fire had started when a spark from a passing locomotive landed on the slanting west roof of the house. A rainless summer had made the shingles and roof as dry as tinder. Attracted by the scarlet sky, neighbors came to do what they could, but no water was available to check the flames.

Five-year-old Cassie Crane, who lived on what is now Lorraine Drive, came to the fire with her family. Ninety years later she told me that she recalled that clear summer night. She remembered lying on the ground across the road, watching sparks fly. She was wrapped in a coat, and someone gave her Parke Avery's pet chicken to hold.

Once his family was safe, James D. Avery remembered the town records. All abstracts and road charts on his desk had burned immediately. Fortunately, land records and vital records with minutes of town meetings were stored in two large, supposedly fireproof safes. It took four days before the safes cooled sufficiently to be investigated.

On Tuesday, July 24, an expert from New York opened the safes. Inside were thirty-four record volumes dating to 1703, the earliest written on parchment. Miraculously, the contents of both safes were found to be in good condition, although the leather bindings had crumbled from the heat.

Town selectmen arranged to have all books repaired and rebound. These volumes are still in use in the Groton Town Hall. In the earliest volume, a few charred fragments of pages are carefully bound in, but fortunately the collection escaped total destruction.

In the wave of nostalgia following the loss of the old Hive of the Averys, the Avery Memorial Association was organized. The homestead's last occupant, James D. Avery, deeded the homesite by the train tracks to the association. The property became a small park. A low curbing preserved the outline of the house, the old hearthstones were set in place and doorways were marked with stone steps. The ancient well sweep was preserved in the rear. In the center, a cylindrical stone obelisk was erected. At the base, a bronze tablet displayed a bas-relief of the homestead. This was a gift of John D. Rockefeller, an Avery descendant on his mother's side.

In July 1900, the Avery Association topped the shaft with a bronze bust of James Avery created by sculptor Bela Pratt, also an Avery descendant.

The Avery Memorial Association still maintains this tiny cleared area by the railroad tracks in Poquonnock. Here the Hive of the Averys once stood, and here the many descendants of James Avery preserve the memory of their distinguished ancestor.

GROTON'S INCORPORATION DAY

The town of Groton observed its 300th anniversary in 2005 with a special celebration on May 10, the date of its incorporation.

In 1705, Groton became a separate town after being known for decades as the "east side" of Pequot Plantation or New London, founded by John Winthrop Jr. in 1646. Settlers from Massachusetts had peopled the colony on the deep harbor of the Thames.

Families were attracted across the river by the fine, level land of Poquonnock Plains, gradually making their homes some distance from the center of New London. However, there was one problem with living on the east side. Residents had to plod over rough trails every Sunday to attend the established church in the mother settlement across the river. Even in stormy weather, they were forced to cross the wide Thames on Cary Latham's ferry. In winter, especially, it was a hardship.

Almost at once they pleaded for separation from New London. As early as 1678, James Avery appealed to the legislature, stating that twenty-eight families lived on the east side, some traveling six or seven miles to the ferry crossing every Sabbath. He asked that they be allowed to have their own church, but New London was reluctant to let them go.

The dedication of the Groton Town Hall, a gift of Morton F. Plant, September 17, 1908.

After nine years they were grudgingly permitted to invite the minister to the west side every third Sunday in the inclement season. In May 1696, the General Court went further, allowing west-side inhabitants to organize an independent church. They chose Ephraim Woodbridge as their minister, and on May 27, 1703, they raised their meetinghouse at the four corners in Center Groton, now the junction of North Road and Route 184. This was actually the geographic center of town at that time, for originally Groton stretched north from the Sound to Poquetannuck, including what is today the town of Ledyard.

It was icing on the cake when their status was legalized on May 5, 1705, and the General Court granted full independence to the new town. They christened it Groton after the Winthrop estate in England. Hardhearted New London had finally agreed to the separation, insisting on a long list of requirements to make up the financial loss that independence would cause.

Groton had to pay a portion of New London's debts, and the ferry and profit from its use would remain the property of New London. The west side could still cut masts or timber in Groton's pine swamp, and any property given to the ministry of New London would remain in its possession forever. It was a hard bargain, but Groton had cut the apron strings and was independent at last.

Written for the Groton Tercentennial Committee

BARE BONES OF THE AVERYS

From the early days in Pequot Plantation, the Averys were a force to be reckoned with. James Avery Sr. appeared in town from Massachusetts about 1651, purchasing land east of the Thames River in the Poquonnock area "on the plain next to Skull Plain" about 1657.

Two years later, he added grants bought from Jarvis Mudge, and later a tract from John Coite, until he owned more than fifty acres stretching from Great Brook to the landmark "three rocks." In terms of Groton's present geography, his property lay north of Route 1, reaching from near the Avery-Morgan Cemetery to the Claude Chester School driveway, where the remains of the three rocks may still be seen adjoining Groton's Poquonnock Plains Park. Somewhere east of the brook he built his house and made his home.

James Sr.'s sons became prominent in town affairs. When his eldest, James Jr., married Edward Stallion's daughter Debora, Stallion gave the couple a farm with a house and barn that he owned in Birch Plain, lying to the southwest of James Sr.'s house. This property today is just south of the junction of Route 1 and Poquonnock Road below the railroad overpass, the site of the Avery Memorial. This old house, with additions through the years,

The bones of Captain Samuel Avery, Groton's first townsman, ready to be reinterred in 1923. *Courtesy of Jim Streeter.*

became the famous Hive of the Averys. It brimmed over with family members until it burned in 1894, set afire by a spark from a passing locomotive.

Many people will tell you, including members of the Avery Family Association, that James Sr. built the Hive of the Averys and that he lived there. Do not believe them. He had his own house to the eastward. All this is proved by reference to Groton Probate and Land Records.

Samuel, the youngest of his four sons, reported that James Sr. lived on "the farm where I now dwell, bounded on the east and partly on the south by the brook or river and part of the salt cove and on the south with the lane that parts this land and the farm of Major John Winthrop." That lane is now Route 1. Winthrop's farm is the present Bluff Point Coastal Reserve. The senior Avery died on April 18, 1700, and Samuel inherited his father's farm, just a bit east of his brother James's Hive of the Averys.

Samuel, although the youngest, was no shrinking violet. He played a leading part in Groton affairs as town clerk, justice of the peace and four-time representative of Groton in the General Court, the equivalent of our state legislature. He was active in the militia, too—the colonial army. Commissioned as an ensign in 1705, by 1716 he had advanced to captain. His greatest honor came when Groton became independent. At the first town meeting in December 1705, the town fathers chose Samuel to be first townsman or selectman, responsible for all town affairs.

Samuel spent his later years in Groton's North Parish, now Ledyard, and there he died on May 1, 1723. He was buried in Ledyard, and the site of his last resting place was forgotten.

An ancient cemetery in Groton, not far from Samuel's home, had existed through the years. Nearby, another early Groton settler, James Morgan, had built his house. In 1923, descendants of these two hardy colonists launched an effort to restore this ancient burial ground of their ancestors, cleaning and resetting the stones. Leading the effort was one of Captain Samuel's descendants, A.W. Pierson of Niagara Falls, New York. He had interested another of Samuel's descendants, someone who had made good in the business world—John D. Rockefeller. With Pierson as his representative, Rockefeller agreed to finance the restoration.

Pierson, with the aid of Percival Morgan of Mystic, located the forgotten grave of Captain Samuel Avery in a deserted cemetery on the Ledyard farm of C.H. Stanton. They opened the grave, finding that nothing remained of the coffin, but Samuel's skull and bones were in good condition. They placed them in a new coffin and removed him to the Avery-Morgan Cemetery in Poquonnock, where he was reinterred ceremoniously beside his wife Susanna, who had died in 1747. A Groton genealogist, Lucy Morgan Adams, was present with her camera. Lucy had traced her roots to the Avery and Morgan families. Taking advantage of this great photo op, she photographed his bones.

In October 1924, a year later, the *Hartford Daily Times* reported the reburial in Poquonnock. Avery's stone in the new location reads, "Here lyeth the body of Capt. Samuel Avery, Esq, who died May 1, 1723. Groton 1st Townsman & Moderator." On the reverse it notes, "Removed from Ledyard cemetery Oct. 17, 1923. by John D. Rockefeller and Albert W. Pierson, Descendants of the 11th Generation."

WHITEFIELD THE EVANGELIST VISITS GROTON

When the legendary English evangelist the Reverend George Whitefield (pronounced Whitfield) visited New England in 1740–41, religious fervor swept the land, ushering in the revival known as the Great Awakening, which shook existing churches to their foundations.

Whitefield crossed the Atlantic seven times during his ministry. Everywhere, he was greeted by vast crowds of listeners. Churches were too small to hold the throngs who came, so he spoke in the open air. His name has been all but forgotten today, but during his lifetime, this eloquent man preached several times in Stonington and Groton. Exact locations where he addressed the multitudes were pointed out as historic spots for decades.

Born in Gloucester, England, in 1714, the son of an innkeeper, George Whitefield attended Oxford University, where he was associated with John Wesley, the founder of Methodism. During this period, religious indifference prevailed in England and America, but Whitefield became convinced that he should promote a revival of piety. He began to preach near Oxford, appealing for support for charity schools.

He was a born actor with a keen dramatic sense. His sermons attracted large audiences, whether he spoke at early dawn or late at night. When churches could not contain the crowds, he moved to the open fields.

The Whitefield Elm in Stonington under which the evangelist preached, from a 1949 postcard.

Despite his youthful appearance, the rich tones of his majestic voice made him a spellbinder. People gladly parted with their money for his cause. "His words are as arrows of a skillful archer sent home to the heart," wrote one listener.

In 1736, Whitefield was ordained by the Church of England. He followed the Wesley brothers across the ocean to Georgia in 1738, returning to England later to raise funds for a Georgia orphanage. With his popular open-air preaching, he soon had £1,000. Back in America, he laid the cornerstone of this orphanage, called Bethesda, in March 1740, providing beds for forty children and feeding one hundred daily.

Then the evangelist traveled up the East Coast of the United States, preaching in major cities and making his way to Boston, where so great was his fame that crowds came out to meet him miles from the city.

Whitefield returned to England suffering from poor health, but he continued his preaching even when his work was harshly criticized by the standing order. In 1745, he was again in New England, and according to Joshua Hempstead's diary, he visited Groton.

On August 8, 1745, the diarist wrote, "Went to Stonington & stopt a while at Groton meetinghouse to see Mr. Whitefield." On Sunday the eleventh he recorded, "Ye Revd Mr. George Whitefield preached again all day under the oak tree in ye forenoon. Stood in his Chair took off his horse…a great assembly perhaps twice So many as could possibility Sitt in ye meetinghouse…an Excellent preacher." Joshua went to East Lyme the next day to hear the evangelist once more.

Whitefield's popularity in America never faded. In 1747, he preached in Stonington at the site opposite the Center Church at the junction of Pequot Trail and Taugwonk Road. The great elm tree under which he stood was ever afterward known as the Whitefield Elm. At the time of the Stonington Tercentennial in 1949, a postcard was published showing this historic tree.

In 1758, the Groton Congregational Church installed a new minister, the Reverend Jonathan Barber, a former associate of Whitefield who had worked at the Georgia orphanage from 1740 to 1746. In June 1763, the famous preacher came once more to New England on his way from Georgia to Boston and promised to visit his old friend Jonathan Barber.

Barber spread the news and hurried to prepare for the coming. He lived in the old parsonage built in 1704 at the crossroads in Center Groton, near the present intersection of Daboll Road and Route 117 and close to the first Groton meetinghouse. To accommodate Whitefield, Barber erected a scaffold or platform, extending from the second floor of his parsonage, where the evangelist could stand high above his audience.

From all over the country people came to the Groton crossroads to hear the Englishman preach. Some traveled all night to be there. Crowds thronged the old Post Road, now Route 184.

At 10:00 a.m., Whitefield appeared on his platform, stepping through the window of the upper bedchamber. The crowd was eager to hear this man who was known as the greatest pulpit orator of the century. They listened and begged for more. When it was time for him to leave, a multitude on foot and horseback accompanied his carriage to the Groton ferry.

Three years later, Whitefield died of asthma at Newburyport, Massachusetts, on September 30, 1770. Only the day before, he had preached for two hours at Exeter, New Hampshire. During his lifetime, he delivered more than eighteen thousand sermons.

The old Barber house in Center Groton was pointed out for years as the place where Whitefield preached. When it burned to the ground in 1924, newspapers recalled the 1767 visit of the evangelist.

THE FIRST BAPTIST CHURCH IN CONNECTICUT

Anniversaries abound these days. New London's 350th occurred in 1996, with Stonington's three years later. Mystic celebrated its 350th in 2004.

The parsonage of the first Baptist church in Connecticut, established in 1704.

The year 2005 marked the town of Groton's tercentennial. We live where history was made, and there are many dates to observe.

Along with Mystic's anniversary, the year 2004 marked the tercentennial of the first Baptist church in Connecticut, a church now known as the Old Mystic Baptist Church, located on Shewville Road. There the three-hundred-year-old organization occupies a spacious contemporary building in a pleasantly rural setting.

In 1704, a year before Groton was separated from New London, twelve dissenters from the established church petitioned the General Court of Connecticut, asking to be allowed to establish their own congregation. The document, dated October 5, 1704, and signed by six men and six women, read in part,

> *We differ from you in Som Poynts of Religion but yet we desire to Live Peasably and quietly with our Neighbors...we understand that your law requires us to Petition to you for the settling of our Meeting and we humbly submit thereto and do beseech of you that you would not deny us...We do desier that our meeting might be stated and held at Will Starks in New London.*

This was a courageous document, unusual for the time. Six women signed at a time when women's names were rarely affixed to legal documents. And although denomination is not mentioned, those who signed were Baptists, radically differing from the colony's accepted and established church.

Connecticut was settled by Puritans whose ministers were in firm control of both church and state. Baptists believed in a separation of the two. The Massachusetts Bay Colony had booted out Roger Williams when he dared to differ, and he had fled to Rhode Island in 1636. That colony became a shelter for all who were distressed in conscience and clashed with the government. Williams established the first Baptist Church in America in Providence in 1639.

In the colonies' early years, Baptists were outcasts, rejected because they objected to the established order. This attitude was a holdover from England, where Baptists had been persecuted since Henry VIII found them distasteful. Other monarchs followed his example. Baptists were branded on the forehead with hot irons, publicly whipped in the city streets or turned out of their homes into open country. A number were burned at the stake, including John Rogers during the reign of Queen Mary and Edward Wightman, the last martyr under King James who died in the Litchfield marketplace in 1611.

Those who signed the 1704 petition—local residents but probably members of a Rhode Island church—included Daniell Pierse, minister; Sergeant William Stark; John Culver; and Isaac Lamb. They were surely courageous. The General Court could have taken grave offense, but that did not happen. Actually, their petition was ignored. They never received an answer. Interpreting silence as consent, they went ahead and held their meetings, assembling at what we now call Old Mystic, a safe distance from New London's ministry. The next year they called Valentine Wightman from North Kingston, Rhode Island, to be their pastor. Will Stark deeded Wightman a house with twenty acres of land. This building was celebrated in the twentieth century as "the oldest Baptist parsonage in America" until it burned in 1936. The Baptists built their meetinghouse at the top of what is now Cold Spring Road "at the burying ground," now Wightman Cemetery.

This lone Baptist congregation flourished, partly because Groton's contemporary established ministers, the Reverend Ephraim Woodbridge and the Reverend John Owen, were friendly with Valentine Wightman. Apparently they believed in religious liberty. Owen interceded for the Baptists on several occasions and was himself censured by the established church.

Three centuries ago, a dozen brave souls visualized their own church, daring to differ from the rest of the town. Their church was a vital factor in the creation of many other Baptist churches in the state. Their vision has gone far.

JOHN LEDYARD THE TRAVELER

When we consider the significant people born in Groton, we must not forget John Ledyard the Traveler. He was world famous in his day, but he has been woefully neglected in the town of his birth. Hopefully plans are under way to remedy that.

He was born near Groton Heights in 1751, the son of sea captain John Ledyard. The Ledyards were prominent in town. His uncles William and Ebenezer became heroes at Fort Griswold in 1781. The lad grew up near the Thames River, a happy childhood that ended abruptly when his father died at sea of malaria when John was ten years old. Later, his widowed mother moved to Long Island, sending him to live with his grandfather, Squire John Ledyard, in Harford. Never again was John's life secure and happy.

Eventually, he enrolled in the newly formed Dartmouth College, arriving flamboyantly in a sort of chariot and making a lasting impression, though he failed to distinguish himself scholastically. By the spring of 1773, he had had enough of college.

John felled a huge tree and hallowed it out in Native American fashion, making a dugout in which he paddled down the Connecticut River to his grandfather's house in Harford. This pilgrimage has become a hallowed

Hawaiian natives greet Captain Cook in this old woodcutting. Groton native John Ledyard was part of this expedition.

Ledyard traveled in Kamschatka on his voyage with Captain James Cook.

part of Dartmouth tradition, and there are memorials on campus recalling Ledyard and his canoe journey.

After dropping out of college, John failed, in turn, at law, teaching and the ministry, and in desperation he went to sea. He eventually signed on with Captain Cook in England for the explorer's final round-the-world voyage. As corporal of the marines, he traveled to the northwest coast of North America, where he was impressed with the potential of the fur trade. He later convinced Thomas Jefferson of the importance of this territory. When Jefferson became president, he sent Lewis and Clark exploring to America's West Coast.

Later, in Hawaii, Cook was killed by the natives, and the expedition made it back to England without him. Ledyard had kept a journal on the voyage, but his notes were confiscated by the admiralty. However, he found his way back home across the Atlantic and wrote a version of his adventures from memory. He sold the manuscript to a Hartford publisher for twenty guineas, so he didn't benefit when it became a runaway bestseller.

This colorful man became an international celebrity in his day, making headlines wherever he went. He was well acquainted with the famous—men such as Jefferson, Benjamin Franklin and John Paul Jones. Yet he was always unlucky. He failed to find a financial backer for developing trade in the Northwest.

Eventually, in desperation, he attempted to walk across Siberia in the dead of winter, hoping to cross the Bering Strait to reach this land of opportunity, but he was arrested and deported as a spy on the orders of Russian Empress Catherine. Next he was employed to explore the hidden sources of the Nile in Africa. Sadly, he died there of fever in 1789.

Largely forgotten through the years, this impetuous character is finally getting some attention. Three great books about him have been published recently. The first, *American Traveler*, is a fine biography by Dartmouth graduate James Zug. A companion volume of Ledyard's journals published by *National Geographic*, entitled *The Last Voyage of Captain Cook: The Collected Writings of John Ledyard*, came out at the same time. Mystic's Flat Hammock Press brought out a fine edition of Jared Sparks's biography *The Life of John Ledyard the American Traveler*, published originally in 1828. This book also contains an afterword by David Anderson, who recently retraced Ledyard's Siberian journey. At last people are paying attention to the life of Groton's native son.

Dartmouth has its memorials to the traveler, and there is even one at Coos Bay in Oregon. Hopefully his native town will soon have a modest marker of its own. Plans are in the works for a boulder bearing a plaque dedicated to this unusual man to be located on the grounds of Bill Memorial Library above the Thames River, which he loved. He was the first great American explorer and deserves some recognition in the town of his birth.

Written for Groton's Tercentennial Committee.

CLOUDS OF WAR

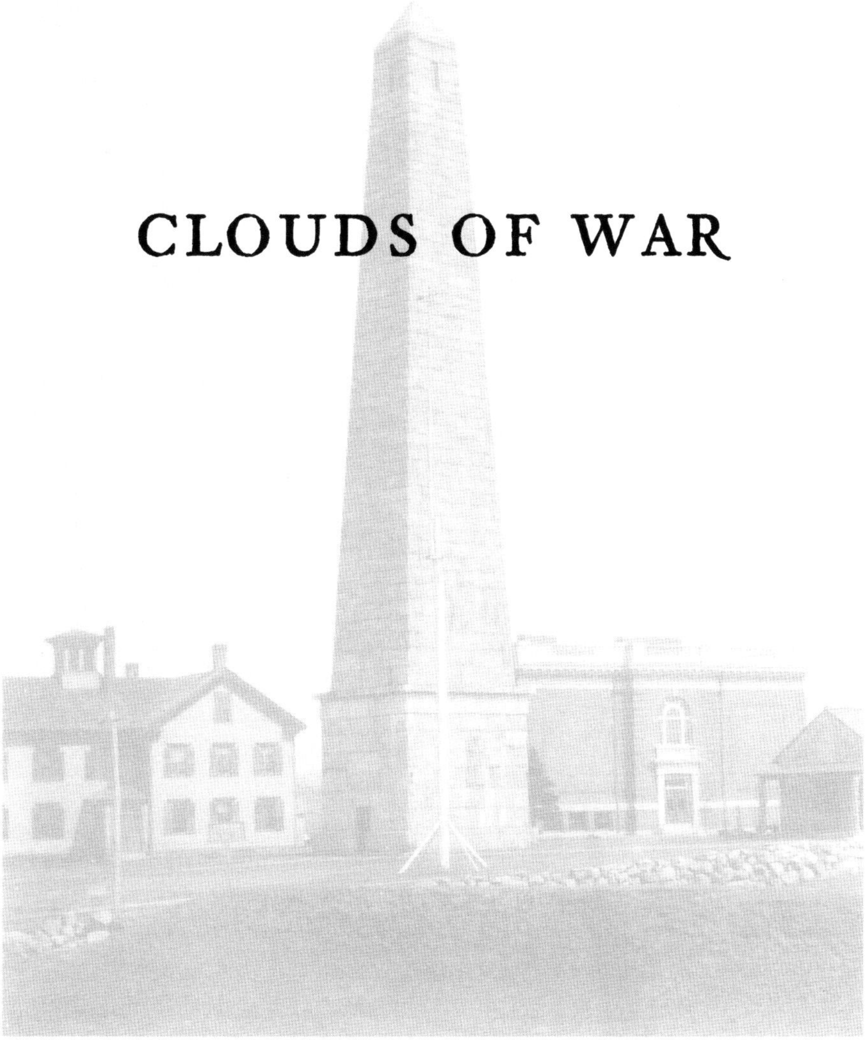

A BRUTAL FREEDOM BATTLE

Groton's Darkest Day

More than two centuries ago, on September 6, 1781, our region suffered a critical enemy invasion when His British Majesty's forces, led by the traitor Benedict Arnold, attacked Fort Griswold and New London. For more than five long, weary years of war, the area around the Thames River had felt safe from this sort of action, and the attack came as a total surprise. It was the eighteenth-century equivalent of 9-11, and its consequences were felt far and wide in the countryside.

At daybreak Sergeant Rufus Avery, who had been in charge of Fort Griswold during the night, saw an enemy fleet lying off New London and summoned his superior officers, Captain William Latham and Colonel William Ledyard. They ordered the alarm to call the militia to defend the fort. We all know of the botched signal and the dreadful battle that followed, observed by Arnold from the safety of Ye Ancientest Burial Ground in New London.

When the alarm was sounded, all able-bodied men hurried to the fort, hastily making what arrangements they could for the safety of their families and valuable possessions. Colonel Ledyard put his wife Anna, with their newborn son and the two younger children, aboard a sailing vessel for Norwich. Those in the vicinity of Groton Heights quickly packed what they could and hastened into the countryside, away from the battlefield. In New London, Jonathan Brooks's father made arrangements for his wife and children to go to Cohanzie, although he remained behind to defend the town.

In these times of technology, it is hard for us to comprehend the lack of communication in those days—no radio, no cellphones, no television coverage. There were no war correspondents to give accounts of the hostilities like those we receive from Afghanistan and Iraq. News traveled by word of mouth from eyewitnesses, and friends and families of the defenders of Fort Trumbull and Fort Griswold had no way of knowing what was happening except by what they saw and heard.

They knew when the battle began by the sound of cannon and musket fire, and they soon saw flames and smoke when the British set fire to stores

The original Groton monument erected in 1830. For the battle centennial in 1881, the height was increased to 134 feet.

and ships in New London and later in Groton. The battle itself lasted only forty minutes, but smoke from burning buildings was visible for hours. Dr. Avery Downer in Preston later wrote, "The smoke from New London appeared like a cloud."

A number of Groton Bank residents gathered in Pleasant Valley at the home of their minister, the Reverend Aaron Kinne, who had come to the church in 1767. There they waited anxiously, not knowing what was happening at the fort. Another group gathered at Fort Hill, where they could see the smoke and hear the shooting. When the firing stopped, they still did not dare venture to the fort. They had no way of knowing whether the British had taken control of the town.

They did not know that in the dark of night the enemy had loaded its prisoners aboard its vessels and left the area, leaving behind the badly wounded on the hard floor of Ensign Ebenezer Avery's house, as well as dozens of dead and dying on the field of battle, including Colonel William Ledyard.

It was daylight when teenaged Anna Warner left the Candlewood Hill farm of her uncle Philip Mills, bound for the fort to determine his fate in the battle. It was morning when Fanny Ledyard, a visitor from

Long Island, made her way to the Avery house and began to minister to the wounded. In those short hours since Sergeant Avery first viewed the enemy force off the harbor, the world had changed for the people of Groton and New London.

Quietly people made their way to Fort Griswold to bring home their wounded or their dead. Stephen Hempstead from New London was badly wounded in the hip. He had been beside Colonel Ledyard at the surrender. Stephen was taken from the Avery house, not to his own home, for that had been burned to the ground, but to his brother's house, where he lay for eleven months "as helpless as a child."

Most adult male members of Groton's First Church had been killed. It was said that there was no one to pass the collection plate the following Sunday. Every family had its losses, and the community was given over to grief and resentment at the work of the traitor Arnold.

Of the 155 defenders in Fort Griswold, 88 were killed, 35 seriously wounded and paroled and 28 taken prisoner. It was a high toll to pay for freedom, and it happened right there on Groton Heights above the Thames River. It is heartening that each year the Friends of Fort Griswold Battlefield and the Anna Warner Bailey Chapter of the Daughters of the American Revolution mark the anniversary of this fatal day with appropriate ceremonies. We must not forget that freedom has a high price.

THE EBENEZER AVERY HOUSE

After the Battle

Ebenezer Avery plied his trade as tailor in a fine two-story house overlooking the Thames River. He also served as ensign in the local militia. On the dark day of September 6, 1781, when the alarm for battle sounded, Ebenezer left his home early in the morning, rushing up the hill to Fort Griswold to help prepare the defense. At day's end, the victorious British returned him to his house, where he lay on the floor severely wounded with fellow Americans, all victims of the massacre following Colonel Ledyard's surrender.

The Groton monument showing two schools, the old wooden Groton Heights School at left, and the newer brick school built in 1912 at right. *Courtesy of Jim Streeter.*

Outnumbered by the enemy, when the battle ended Americans were at the mercy of their foe. When fighting and looting stopped, the British prepared to return to their vessels in the harbor. The captured, walking wounded, were ordered to march down to the riverbank to embark.

According to eyewitness Sergeant Rufus Avery, the British

> *loaded up our very large heavy ammunition wagon with the wounded men who could not go themselves, and about twenty of the soldiers drew the wagon out of the fort and brought it to the brow of the hill on which the fort stood. As soon as the enemy began to move the wagon down the hill they found it too much for them; they released their hold on the wagon…leaving it to run down the hill with great speed. It ran about twelve rods to a large apple tree stump and both shafts of the wagon struck very hard and hurt the wounded men very much.*

It was then that Rufus realized, "I was in the power of a cruel foe or enemy."

The British had planned to load these gravely wounded men as prisoners aboard their ships for New York, but Ebenezer Ledyard, brother of the colonel, came forward and offered to go as hostage in their place if the wounded were spared. Through his valor, the suffering men were taken to the house that Ebenezer Avery had left earlier that day. The invaders had already set it on fire, but the flames were extinguished and the wounded were left lying on the floor unattended. Among them was the ensign himself, severely injured by a shot through the lower part of the neck that cut the cords and left him as senseless as one of the dead.

Also among the wounded was Stephen Hempstead, who later wrote,

> *Such a night of distress and anguish was scarcely ever passed by mortal. Thirty-five of us were lying on the bare floor, stiff, mangled and wounded in every manner, exhausted with pain, fatigue and loss of blood, without clothes or anything to cover us, trembling with cold…*

When the enemy had gone, Dr. Downer and Dr. Prentiss came to attend the wounded men. In the morning, Miss Fanny Ledyard of Southold, Long Island, who was visiting her uncle Colonel Ledyard, brought them warm chocolate and wine and other refreshment.

"We were a horrible sight at this time," wrote Hempstead. "Our own friends did not know us. Even my own wife came in search of me and did not recognize me."

Ensign Ebenezer Avery recovered from his wounds with the loss of his hearing. He lived for many years in the house near the river. He died on January 11, 1828, at the age of eighty-one. But evidences of the battle remained—bloodstains on the floor of his great room where the wounded had lain. During his lifetime, the ensign never allowed them to be washed away.

For nearly two centuries, Avery's house stood at the corner of Latham and Thames Streets, revered as a relic of the Revolution, bearing a sign over the front door explaining that it was here where the wounded lay after the battle. According to local legend, those bloodstains were still visible on the floor. But as traffic and congestion increased, the house was threatened by the encroaching world.

In 1971, through a member of the Avery Family Association, Ensign Ebenezer Avery's house was removed to a safer location up the hill, near the fort that its owner had so bravely defended. It stands there today, cared for by the Averys, resplendent in fresh paint and enhanced by period flower gardens planted by the Trillium Garden Club. Unfortunately, the bloodstains are no longer visible on the floor. When the structure was moved, it was necessary to replace the old timbers. But the house and its nicely furnished rooms are a tangible reminder of sacrifices made in the dark days of the Revolution, when our country won its freedom.

It is interesting to note that there were two Ebenezer Averys at Fort Griswold. The second, Lieutenant Ebenezer Avery, who was killed on the field of battle, lies in Colonel Ledyard Cemetery. His beautifully carved stone reads, "In Memory of Lieut. Ebenezer Avery who fell Gloriously in Defense of fort Griswould [*sic*] and American Freedom Sept. 6th 1781 in ye 49th year of his Age."

BRITISH BLOCKADE STRANGLED GROTON IN THE WAR OF 1812

Those who enjoyed summer sun and sand at the City of Groton's beach might be surprised to learn that during the War of 1812 that Eastern Point shore was closely patrolled by British warships enforcing a grim blockade of the American coast. Designed to bring the youthful nation of the United States to its knees, this vigilant blockade soon ruined Yankee maritime trade and brought hard times to the seafaring communities of New London, Groton, Mystic and Stonington.

The situation worsened in May 1813, when a strong British naval force chased Commodore Stephen Decatur's small American squadron into New London Harbor. Decatur commanded two frigates, *Macedonian* and *United States*, and the sloop of war *Hornet*, representing about one-third of the United States Navy at the time.

Groton and New London residents recalled with alarm the British attack of September 6, 1781. With the enemy at hand, they expected immediate hostile invasion, but the dreaded assault never came. The British found it simpler to tighten their rigid blockade of the south shore and the harbor, keeping Decatur's little fleet out of action with no risk of battle causalities.

During the War of 1812, British warships rigorously blockaded the Thames River harbor, strangling seafaring commerce.

British warships strengthened their patrol of the coast. The powerful HMS *Ramillies*, seventy-four guns, anchored boldly off Eastern Point. Any Yankee vessel venturing out from Mystic, Noank, Groton, New London or another nearby harbor invited capture. Even fishermen were pursued. After British barges boldly entered the Mystic River, the Americans posted detachments of militia along the shore. Sentries were on duty each night in Groton and in Mystic, and Fort Rachel came into being.

Groton and Mystic men made their living from the sea. They chafed under blockade restrictions, which cut off their thriving coastal trade and put an end to prosperity. Ordinary business was suspended by the war.

Gathering in taverns to discuss the news, they learned of the experiments of one Mr. Riker of New York. Riker filled the small sloop *Eagle* with gunpowder, turpentine and tar, and flammable cargo triggered to explode if the hold was opened for inspection. Off New London, the *Eagle* succeeded in blowing up an investigating barge from HMS *Ramillies*, but the detested warship continued its vigil off the mouth of the Thames.

By the spring of 1814, seventeen Mystic men were tired of cooling their heels on land. Pooling their money, they bought their own barge, a single-bank rowing galley powered by sixteen oars. They planned to outfit this small craft with another of Ricker's experiments—a torpedo—hoping to destroy an enemy vessel on blockade duty.

Their leader was Captain Jeremiah Holmes, who had good reason to hate the British. As a young man he had been impressed on a British man-of-war and forced to serve three years of imprisonment on their gunnery crew before he managed to escape. He returned to Mystic, where he commanded a packet sailing between New York and Mystic until the blockade interfered.

Crafty Captain Holmes sneaked his packet past the enemy to New York to get the secret weapon. The torpedo was described by Frederic Denison, writing in the *Mystic Pioneer* in 1859, as a tube thirty feet long and seven inches in diameter. At one end was a twelve-foot crossbar hung with hooks that would fasten into any object they touched. At a certain angle a spring would set off the explosion.

Holmes avoided capture and returned with the torpedo. Before the first attempt, he and his men conferred with Commodore Decatur. One dark night they located HMS *Ramillies* off Fishers Island, but when they tried to launch their torpedo, the rope fouled on the bottom and the lethal weapon sank. To raise it would be suicide, so they cut the rope and abandoned it.

Jeremiah Holmes went back to New York for two more torpedoes. For the next trial, the Mystic men waited until the *Ramillies* was anchored at its favorite spot off Groton's Eastern Point. Protected by darkness, the Americans rowed silently around the enemy warship. They sent out the torpedo and tried to swing it against the hull, but the rope caught on the warship's cable with enough force to set off a loud explosion.

Tons of water flew high in the air. The aroused British crew fired at the little barge. Holmes and his men rowed frantically for the Groton shore and managed to scramble safely from the barge onto Eastern Point. Here they were in more danger from friendly fire as their own sentries began to shoot, but in time they were able to identity themselves.

After this alarm, the British kept such a tight guard against further torpedo attacks that Holmes and the others knew it was useless to try again. The last torpedo was finally returned unused to Riker.

Although the gallant Mystic crew did not achieve their goal, their risky stunt did impress the enemy. A few months later, on August 10, 1814, the British attacked Stonington by sea. One of the conditions they imposed for ending the bombardment was a demand that no torpedoes be outfitted in the village.

THE EPIC BATTLE AT GROTON LONG POINT

Groton Long Point is famous for summer fun; a paradise of sun and sand and sparkling blue waters. Who would think of it as a battle scene? Yet bullets flew in the summer of 1814, when the United States was at war with Great Britain and British warships patrolled the sound, blockading southern Connecticut and destroying its prosperous maritime trade. British sailors captured unwary American vessels that ventured from port, causing unhappiness and unrest in seaport villages. Adding to these indignities, British ships attacked Stonington in August 1814, bombarding the village from offshore. They were turned away only by determined militia.

At that time Groton Long Point was purely rural, having once been part of a major land grant to John Winthrop Jr. (founder of Pequot Plantation) known as Fort Hill Farm. No one was enjoying the sea breezes in August 1814, unless it was the sea gulls. Development as a summer resort was far in the future. The shore lay bare and inviting under summer skies.

A Yankee plot, hatched by idle mariners, came to fruition on August 14, 1814, the day after the triumph at Stonington. Having seen the ponderous eighty-four-gun warship *Ramillies* take flight, the hardy seamen planned a ruse to cause the enemy more discomfort. They decided to decoy and capture a vessel from the British fleet lying in the sound off the hummocks, hoping to lure it away from its protection.

In an 1814 plot against invading British, Mystic troops hid along the east shore of Groton Long Point, shown here in a 1930 photograph. *Courtesy of Jim Streeter.*

They had their eyes on a barge, a type of open boat employed in naval service alongshore. Powered by oars, it was usually fitted with auxiliary sails. Useful for small boat attacks and hit-and-run raids, a barge was furnished with weather cloths all around to mask the crew from small arms fire when in action. Some barges were double enders like large whaleboats, while others had square sterns. Most carried a single gun. British barges of this type had entered the Mystic River, Groton's eastern boundary, capturing the local sloop *Fox* and carrying it off to convert into an enemy privateer.

The seamen in Mystic united to lay plans for the capture, led in their daring by Captain Eldredge Packer. Several squads of militiamen, lately defenders of Stonington, answered the call. A company of eighty eager volunteers rallied under Packer's command to march overland through fields and woods to Groton Long Point, where they hid along the bank that is today's East Shore Avenue, facing Noank's Morgan Point. They remained concealed, waiting for a signal from their lookout, Captain John Barber, who was stationed behind a large boulder overlooking the sound. Leaving nothing to chance, another militia company under Captain Jonathan Wheeler was stationed on the west bank.

Back at the mouth of the Mystic River, the plotters fitted out a large fishing boat, loading it with boxes and crates as if planning to run the blockade. Under the command of Captain Simeon Haley, with a crew composed of four seasoned mariners—Paul Burrows, Henry Park, Peter Washington and Ezekiel Tufts—the decoy vessel sailed out of the Mystic River around Long Point, bound westward, and soon attracted the attention of the British off Eastern Point. Just as the plotters had hoped, a barge from the bomb ship *Terror* started in pursuit. The barge was commanded by Lieutenant Chambers and manned by fourteen hardy British seamen.

Haley's vessel pretended to run for New London, but then, with the enemy in hot pursuit, Haley turned tail, and under full sail and oar power, ran straight up onto the east beach of Long Point. His crew fled over the bank to safety.

As soon as the pursuing enemy barge touched the beach, Captain Barber rose from behind his boulder and waved his sword, signaling the troops in ambush to attack. Captain Packer and his men fired on the barge and demanded its surrender. The action was brief, but there were causalities. A man of Scottish descent was killed, shot through the head, and two were wounded. Lieutenant Chambers, badly outnumbered, could only comply with Barber's request, remarking, "I have heard of Yankee tricks, but this is the first that I have experienced."

The prisoners and the captured prize barge went to Mystic. The wounded were tended at Joseph Avery's house, at the foot of Ashbey Street, where they were given excellent care. The dead man was buried with military honors in the old Packer Cemetery beside the former Mystic Ice House site. The remainder of the crew was billeted in the village, awaiting exchange. To show there were no hard feelings, citizens of Mystic presented the vanquished Lieutenant Chambers with a purse of $100 in consideration of his gentlemanly conduct during the affair.

It was a profitable day for the Americans. The victors received prize money of $1,200 in exchange for the barge, and $1,400 for the prisoners, a compensation for the hardships caused by Mr. Madison's War.

Thus went the battle with the British at Groton Long Point nearly two centuries ago. Unlike the earlier Battle of Groton Heights, this time the Americans won.

HER PETTICOAT SWEPT THIS HEROINE TO FAME

Mother Bailey is Groton's most celebrated heroine. Her flannel petticoat rocketed her to fame during the War of 1812, and she became the toast of the nation. Her house still stands on Thames Street in her native town, proudly restored, looking as it did in the days when Mother Bailey and her husband kept their popular tavern there, frequented by navy men from Commodore Decatur's squadron.

She was born Anna Warner on October 11, 1758. Both of her parents died when she was very young, and she went to live with her Grandmother Mills on a Candlewood Hill farm. She grew unusually tall and strong for a girl, able to help her uncle, Edward Mills, with the farm crops and animals.

When the colonies declared independence from England, Anna longed to be a boy to fight the redcoats, but her work was on the farm. Her Uncle Edward was a corporal in the militia, and when the British attacked on September 6, 1781, he hurried to Fort Griswold, leaving behind his wife, a young son and a newborn baby.

Right: Anna Warner "Mother" Bailey in a portrait drawn from life by John Warner Barber.

Below: Mother Bailey's home on Thames Street in Groton, from a 1936 photograph. *Courtesy of Eva L. Butler.*

All day those at Candlewood heard the sound of cannons and saw smoke rising from the battle and the burning homes of Groton and New London. At night the guns stopped, but Edward did not return.

Anna rose at dawn, milked the cows and, without stopping for breakfast, began the three-mile hike to the fort to find her uncle. She hurried barefoot down the highway, now Route 184, a road already crowded with other worried relatives.

She found Edward lying mortally wounded, weak from loss of blood. He begged Anna to bring his family to him so he could see them once more. Anna hurried back to the farm, saddled the horse, boosted up the young wife and little boy and took the baby in her own arms. They made their way to the Avery house to comfort the dying man.

After the heavy losses at Fort Griswold, Anna Warner hated the British more than ever.

In 1783, she married veteran solider Elijah Bailey and they became innkeepers on Groton Bank below the fort, now Thames Street. Mrs. Bailey's hearty manner and outspoken ways made their tavern popular from the start.

President James Madison declared war on England in 1812, and to Anna Warner Bailey, this was a second Independence Day. Her vigorous denunciation of the British attracted many to the inn.

The war was soon very real to Groton and New London. Decatur's fleet scurried into the harbor in June 1813, pursued by enemy warships, and another attack on the towns seemed imminent.

Inhabitants of Groton Bank fled to the backcountry. Mrs. Bailey sent her household goods and prepared to follow. Major Simeon Smith hastily manned Fort Griswold with his militia and inventoried his supplies. He lacked cartridges and flannel for their wadding and sent a messenger down the hill for flannel, but the village seemed deserted.

The discouraged messenger met Mrs. Bailey and told her of his need. In a moment she had loosened her long, flannel petticoat, stepped grandly out of it and presented it with a flourish and a hearty wish that the wadding would do its work well.

Amused bystanders saluted her daring gesture, for in 1813 ladies did not admit to wearing undergarments, much less remove them in public. The messenger carried his prize to the fort, where it was received with cheers.

The British never attacked, content to bottle up American vessels in the harbor, but word of Mother Bailey's impulsive gift spread across the country. Newspapers hailed her as the nation's greatest female Patriot. After the war, a stream of celebrities knocked at her Groton door—

President Monroe in 1817, Lafayette in 1824 and in 1833, President Andrew Jackson and then–Vice President Martin Van Buren.

As her fame increased, visitors flocked to the tavern to hear the lively tale from her own lips. She was as good as a floor show, dancing about the room, singing patriotic tunes and railing at the British. Groton and New London were proud of her, and there was even a patent medicine, Mother Bailey's Soothing Syrup, named in her honor.

On January 19, 1851, when she was ninety-three, as she snoozed in her favorite armchair near an open hearth, Mother Bailey's clothing caught fire and she died within the hour. Her only survivors were cousins, for her title of "mother" was purely honorary.

Today her name is honored by the Anna Warner Bailey Chapter of the Daughters of the American Revolution, whose headquarters are in the Monument House at Fort Griswold. In this museum are many mementos of this unusual lady, including her desk and her snuff mill. Several portraits show her as a stern, elderly woman wearing a demure white cap and collar, not at all like the reckless heroine of 1813. A sketch made from life by B.F. Lossing for his *Pictorial Field Book of the Revolution* catches a softer look.

The most impressive reminder of Groton's Anna Warner Bailey is her stately house at the corner of Thames and Broad Streets. Dingy and deserted for many years, the former tavern was renovated and restored by Robert and Tanya Artinian to begin a new career.

Mother Bailey would love the way her house looks now.

THE VALENTINE'S DAY IRONCLAD

On Valentine's Day 1862, an ironclad gunboat was launched at the Maxson Fish and Company shipyard in West Mystic in Groton. This strange vessel, the Union navy's new secret weapon against the Confederacy, was hailed as a bombproof steamer that could pulverize the strongest enemy vessels. This was our navy's second ironclad. The famous *Monitor* was its first. After the battle of Hampton Roads on March

The USS *Galena* ironclad gunboat launched at West Mystic on February 14, 1862, from the Maxson Fish shipyard.

The USS *Galena* in later years after rebuilding. The vessel served in the navy until 1891. *Courtesy of the National Archives.*

9, 1862, *Monitor* and *Merrimack* became household words, but our second ironclad, the USS *Galena*, is seldom mentioned.

The shipyard at West Mystic had been building the vessel since the previous September. Work on the ironclad was supervised by Samuel Hartt Pook of Boston, designer of the noted clipper ship *Red Jacket*. He personally selected each piece of timber for the gunboat's frame. All the countryside followed the construction, which was so alien to the town that had built and launched dozens of wooden vessels.

The *Galena*'s design was far more conservative than the *Monitor*'s, the radical cheese box on a raft. The *Galena* was a typical wood vessel whose sides were overlaid with heavy iron armor. Dovetailed iron bars, twelve feet long, two to three inches thick and four inches wide were bolted to the oak frame, held securely with large rivets. Each flanged plate was fastened to form a smooth surface for the hull.

This wooden hull had convex sides that bulged oddly outward, a "tumble-home" that designers believed would reduce strain on the hull when the oceangoing ironclad rolled in rough seas. From a thirty-six-foot width at the waterline, the upper deck narrowed to twenty-six feet across.

In seven weeks the gunboat's wooden frame was ready to receive its armor. The iron rails, rolled by a new process at Winslow's Foundry in Troy, New York, were applied to the hull by factory representatives working with shipyard hands. It was a tricky job, and there were many problems.

At least one hundred workmen swarmed about the Maxson Fish shipyard. Some even worked on Sundays. When cold weather came, carpenters enclosed the gunboat in a huge shed to furnish shelter for those who struggled with the bulky armament.

The village was full of gossip and speculation about the ironclad's chances in the war. Some felt it was a silly project. They reasoned that if a bar of iron could not float, how could an iron-covered ship stay above water?

The nation followed the vessel's progress in *Harper's Weekly*, which twice ran illustrated articles about the bombproof steamer. But Amos Watrous, editor of the *Mystic Pioneer*, warned local readers not to expect too much. He thought iron vessels too rapid a change to succeed, cautioning, "Wise persons distrust efforts made in advance of stereotyped productions."

The ironclad certainly was not stereotyped. Nothing like it had ever been built before. With the pressure of wartime need, it was finally ready for launching on Valentine's Day, 130 days after its keel was laid.

Everyone for miles around planned to attend the launching. There was always a chance that the heavy iron plating might sink the vessel at once, and many thought the clumsy gunboat would founder the moment it took to the water.

Even the shipbuilder's son, Simeon G. Fish, had his doubts. He had worked on the vessel from the start, but as the launch time approached, he grew nervous. On February 13 he wrote in his diary, "By this time tomorrow we shall have a launch or a flummox!"

Many in Groton predicted a flummox, and they rose before dawn on Valentine's Day to reach the river by 9:00 a.m., crowding the shore to see the spectacle. But when launching time came, there was no flummox! At 9:12 a.m. the hope of the Union glided gracefully into the river, proud and upright, scarcely careening in spite of its heavy iron easing. The crowd cheered, and Amos Watrous reported with surprise, "She floats like a duck!"

On Washington's birthday a tug took the ironclad to the Continental Iron Works at Greenpoint, Long Island, where the *Monitor* was built, to fit the vessel for war service. Until this time, the new ironclad had no official name, but on February 25 Simeon Fish wrote in his diary, "Gunboat named *Galena*." No one today knows why the name was chosen, but *Galena* it remained for all its days afloat.

The *Galena* was commissioned in April as a third-rate screw steamer, 738 tons, armed with four nine-inch Dahlgren guns and two one-hundred-pound Parrott rifles. The 180-foot vessel cost the government $247,284.40.

It would be nice to report that the Valentine's Day ironclad lived up to its expectations. Unfortunately, it was outclassed by the *Monitor* and suffered a terrible pounding from Rebel guns at Drewry's Bluff on May 15, 1862. However, the sturdy vessel later served Farragut at Mobile Bay and, after rebuilding, continued in the navy until 1891.

THE COMING OF GROTON'S NAVAL SUBMARINE BASE

Groton's submarine base has been a presence on the east bank of the Thames since 1868, and for much of that time its chances for survival were

The famous escape training tower at the U.S. Naval Submarine Base, built in 1930, was demolished in 1991.

slim. Yet it did survive and eventually flourished. Let this be an omen for the future.

Commodore Stephen Decatur recognized the area's potential as early as 1812, writing, "I wish there might be a naval yard at New London for I know of no other harbor in the United States possessing so many advantages." The site offered both ocean access and safe anchorage in a harbor that seldom froze during winter months. Many agreed about the site's worth, but only after the Civil War did Decatur's wish come true, and then only after much hard work on the part of community leaders.

The American navy had changed greatly during the War Between the States with the introduction of so-called iron vessels to replace wooden hulls and the substitution of steam-powered vessels for sailing ships. Now there was a need for a new navy yard to build and service this innovative fleet. Three ports were in the running. New London was one, along with Narragansett Bay and League Island in the Delaware River. Truthfully, New London was a poor choice, for it was at some distance from the sources of coal and iron the new navy needed. The matter was settled in favor of League Island when the city of Philadelphia offered the site as a free gift to the federal government, cinching the deal.

They lost the first round, but Connecticut Yankees do not give up. Following Philadelphia's example, the Connecticut state legislature furnished money to send lobbyists to Washington and appropriated $15,000 toward the purchase of a site to be presented to the government. New London agreed to match that sum. Protecting their investment, the lobbyists managed to get an act through Congress in March 1867 directing the secretary of the navy to accept any deed offered by Connecticut.

The prime mover at the local level was John R. Bolles, member of the New London Board of Trade and an author and publisher. He had already written several vigorous pamphlets setting forth the advantages of a New London navy yard, printing them at the family printing establishment. He worked tirelessly for the cause and eventually bought up land for the site. Land in New London was expensive, so the east side of the river was chosen. The property included farmland of the Culver, Latham, Chapman, Marshall and Bixby families.

On April 17, 1868, a tract of 112 acres, including one mile of waterfront, was conveyed to the federal government. The New London Navy Yard was finally a reality, although it wasn't in that town at all, but lay across the river in Groton. Through the years it was always called the New London Navy Yard, probably because of that city's financial aid. In fact, some of the news releases at present still call it New London rather than Groton.

New London sat back and waited for prosperity, but the great shipyard for building iron warships never materialized. Congress refused to appropriate funds until 1872, when two brick buildings were constructed. A New London newspaper complained the next year that the naval station was more ornamental than useful, and in 1875 the Senate Committee on Naval Affairs recommended that the yard be abandoned because the channel was too narrow and the saltwater injurious to iron ships. Then came a move to transfer the naval asylum from Philadelphia to the Thames River site.

Year after year the yard was in jeopardy, but it somehow managed to survive as a coaling station for small craft of the Atlantic fleet, although it was far from the promoter's dreams. Not until 1915, when the new submarine service found the site useful, did its luck change. At that point, four small submarines with their tender arrived to begin training in Long Island Sound, returning to the base each night. This was so successful that in 1917 the navy formally commissioned the yard as a submarine base. Five thousand officers and men trained there during World War I, beginning a long period of vital service to the nation.

Though the first half century was insecure, the years that followed allowed the base to come into its own as a prime factor in the nuclear navy, a vital part of the life and economy of the region and a permanent part of the community, reminiscent of John Bolles and others who worked in the early days to bring a navy yard to the Thames River.

THE MARITIME WORLD

THE GIANT TWINS

Groton's Great Steamships

The great sheds and heavy cranes of General Dynamics occupy a long stretch of the eastern or Groton shore of the Thames River, a prime spot for shipbuilding. Before General Dynamics there was the New London Ship and Engine, and before that, in the old North Yard, spidery ways of the Eastern Shipbuilding Company loomed on the horizon. From this site, many vessels have entered the water, but none was more impressive than the enormous sister steamships *Minnesota* and *Dakota*. When they were built, they were the largest steel freighters in the world.

The *Minnesota* was launched in 1903 and the *Dakota* a year later. Each giant vessel displaced twenty-one thousand tons. Each was 622 feet long with a beam of 73 feet—roughly the size of the late Swedish liner *Gripsholm*. They may have been the only American-built vessels equipped with opium dens.

Primarily designed for carrying cargo, each had cabins for 253 first-class passengers and provision for 300 second-class and 2,400 third-class passengers. The possibility of Asiatic passengers or crew prompted the inclusion of opium dens, but in wartime, each ship could be converted into a troop transport or could be used to carry cattle.

These vessels were the dream of railroad tycoon James J. Hill, who had just completed the Great Northern Railroad across the continent to carry wheat products from the Midwest. Now he hoped to transport flour across the Pacific for potential oriental markets. If every Asian ate only one ounce of flour daily, he could sell sixty million bushels of wheat a year.

Hill needed large freighters for this project. He planned to beat construction costs by establishing his own shipyard. Charles R. Hanscom, his superintendent of construction, surveyed the East Coast, and in March 1900 he selected the site on the Groton bank of the Thames that had been used until 1889 for the old railroad ferry.

Hanscom thought it ideal. Solid rock on the shore would bear the freighters' immense weight and deep water was at hand for launching. He built two sets of seven-hundred-foot ways and erected three new buildings. The old brick roundhouse was converted into a power plant.

The giant steamship *Minnesota*, launched by Eastern Shipbuilding Company in Groton on April 16, 1903. *Courtesy of the Public Library of New London.*

Groton and New London hailed Hill's move as the dawn of prosperity. Hordes of workers arrived, creating a business boom and a housing shortage. The village at Groton Bank incorporated as a borough to enable it to furnish electricity and city water for the new shipyard. Things looked rosy, and there was talk of a new electric street railway.

Constructing steel vessels on the banks of the Thames was difficult, but eventually the first vessel, the *Minnesota*, was ready for launching on April 16, 1903. The town declared a holiday. Schools and stores closed and a crowd of forty thousand assembled for the spectacle. Some occupied grandstands and wharves. Others watched from decks of the Sound steamers *Block Island* and *Rhode Island*.

The *Minnesota* was on the ways, its unfinished sister ship *Dakota* beside it. Launching was set for high noon, with J.J. Hill's daughter Clara as sponsor. At twelve on the dot, she climbed the launching platform where the bottle of champagne was ready, stepped forward with bottle in hand and awaited the signal.

It was a cold April day. A brisk northeast breeze buffeted the crowds and chilled them to the bone. With Clara Hill they waited expectantly, but no signal came. Far below, stubborn bilge blocks held the behemoth fast and it refused to budge. One hundred workmen battered timbers to release it, while spectators shivered in Arctic breezes.

It was 2:15 p.m. before the last timber went down. Slowly the huge *Minnesota* began to move down the ways. As the vessel gathered speed, Miss Hill dashed her bottle of champagne just in time.

The ship slid forward, entering the river gracefully while everyone cheered. It floated easily, drawing about twelve feet of water. Then the crowd left for home, sniffling and sneezing.

On February 6, 1904, when the *Dakota* was ready, the weather was even worse. The wintery day held the crowd down to ten thousand and many stood in ankle-deep slush. Fortunately, the second twin went into water without delay.

The *Minnesota* was fitted out and made its first trip to the Orient from Seattle in January 1905, breaking all existing records. The *Dakota* soon joined it on the Pacific. Unfortunately, they were not the success J.J. Hill expected. A worldwide shipping slump followed the Russo-Japanese War. The two vessels carried wheat to the Orient but found few return cargoes.

In March 1907 the *Dakota* was lost near Yokohama. People in Groton expected J.J. Hill to build an immediate replacement. They missed the prosperity brought by Eastern Shipbuilding, but the great yard lay idle. Their hopes were dashed in 1908 when the shipyard was dismantled and the equipment sold at auction. The new borough of Groton faced unemployment and hard times. Tenements lay empty and the depression lasted until 1911, when the old yard was purchased for the New London Ship and Engine.

The *Minnesota* sailed in the Pacific until 1915, the largest and most palatial tourist ship in that part of the world. During World War I, it was converted to a transport and carried troops to England, eluding U-boats during several Atlantic crossings.

THE SAD FATE OF A GIANT SCHOONER

The five-masted *Jennie R. Dubois* was the largest vessel ever built on the Mystic River above Noank, but when the schooner was launched at West Mystic in Groton on February 11, 1902, the huge craft went into the water so smoothly it wouldn't have cracked an egg.

The *Dubois* (pronounced "Du-boys" locally) was built at Oldfield Shipyard, the birthplace of clipper ships and the Civil War ironclad *Galena*. The Holmes Shipbuilding Company reactivated the yard in 1900. William K. Holmes of Wall Street, president of the firm, soon secured a contract from James D. Dewell to build a 249-foot schooner, 46 feet in breadth and 26 in depth, capable of carrying three thousand tons of coal or two million feet of timber in the Dewell coastal fleet.

Master builder W.A. Hodgkins of Bath, Maine, directed the laying of the keel on April 10, 1901. The vessel was built to rigid Lloyd's specifications, with a white oak hull and five-inch planking. Captain Edward Smeed, who was to command it, arrived at West Mystic during the summer to oversee construction.

The launch of the schooner *Jennie R. Dubois* at West Mystic, February 11, 1902.

Month by month, neighbors watched progress on the immense hull. The shipyard lay near railroad tracks, and passengers on the New Haven trains admired the work. By December, workers had fitted the fifty-foot bowsprit and seventy-foot jib boom and began to prepare the launching ways.

At this time the vessel's name was chosen. It was named the *Jennie R. Dubois* in honor of the wife of Rhode Island Judge E.C. Dubois, a Dewell stockholder.

The vessel was to be launched fully rigged. In mid-January 1902, crowds gathered at West Mystic to watch as giant cranes stepped the masts. Five big sticks of Oregon pine, each 108 feet long, were put in position and surmounted by 56-foot topmasts. From stem to stern, the masts were called fore, main, mizzen, jigger and spanker. The Mystic weekly newspaper claimed the schooner was the first five-master built in Connecticut.

The 2,227-ton vessel cost $100,000, the latest word in shipbuilding. The cabin, forecastle and covered wheelhouse were steam heated. In the captain's quarters, heavy Brussels carpet covered the floor and there was a modern bathroom. Interiors were finished in natural wood for an impression of luxury.

The launching, set for high water at 11:00 a.m. on Tuesday, February 11, 1902, was a gala occasion. Standard Machinery Company, Mystic's biggest industry, closed. So did local schools and many stores. Reporters estimated that six thousand persons lined West Mystic shores south of the railroad tracks. Others watched from the hills.

New London's famous Jibboom Club attended in full force along with the Noank Band. Trains brought stockholders from New London, Providence and Stonington. The village of West Mystic had never seen such a holiday crowd.

At 11:05 a.m., the last block was knocked away and the schooner slid forward with a rush. Mrs. Dubois broke a bottle of wine on her namesake's quarter and recited original verses she had written for the occasion:

Lady of the Mystic shrine,
with the flash of sparkling wine,
Prisoned sunshine of the vine,
Gayly decked with streamers fine,
I instruct you to the brine.

There were more lines, but her words were lost as whistles shrieked and spectators cheered. The big schooner entered the water, creating a huge wave that washed over shipyard docks, drenching hundreds, but all agreed it was a most successful launch.

The *Jennie R. Dubois* made a pretty picture on the river, her five tall masts bedecked with flags. Lunch was served aboard to honored guests and the crowd dispersed.

The next morning, workers found the pristine white vessel stuck fast in mud by the narrow channel. The schooner remained there for six days until a heavy snowstorm with stiff northeast winds dislodged it and the *Dubois* floated free, fortunately uninjured by the mishap.

The giant schooner, too large for the Mystic River, grounded again in March on the way to New London to begin its maiden voyage, but on April 2 it left for Baltimore to load coal for Boston, a profitable trade that continued for seventeen months.

On Saturday, September 7, 1903, the *New London Day* reported the sinking of an unidentified vessel off Block Island, topmasts sticking out of the water but no trace of crew wreckage. The mystery was solved when the German tramp steamer *Schonfels* put into New York. The captain reported that on September 5, in a dense fog, the steamer had run into and sunk the schooner *Jennie R. Dubois*. The Germans rescued Captain Smeed and the unfortunate crew, depositing them in New York without a nickel among them.

The steamer had struck the schooner amidship in the fog. Captain Smeed had seen the *Schonfels* approaching a half mile away. He had held his course, sounding his foghorn because the sailing vessel had the right of way. The *Jennie R. Dubois*, carrying three thousand tons of coal, went to the bottom like a stone. The crew barely reached safety. It sank in over eighty feet of water, but its towering masts were a menace to navigation. U.S. engineers had to dynamite them in order to clear the passage.

It was a sad end to the life of the handsome schooner.

WORLD WAR I AND THE GROTON IRON WORKS

Sometimes we are apt to overlook the history of that prime site on the Groton bank of the Thames now occupied by the Pfizer plant. Before Pfizer there was the Victory Yard of the Electric Boat Company, from which many of its seventy-four World War II submarines were delivered to the navy. Before that there was the Atlantic Fisheries, and even before that, during World War I, we had the Groton Iron Works, whose workers overcrowded the town's streets and schools.

Financier Charles S. Morse developed the ironworks shipyard on the Henry C. Rowe estate at Eastern Point. He purchased the property in November 1916, intent on building large steel freighters for the war effort. Vessels were in extraordinary demand, and one successful voyage would pay for the cost of building.

At the same time he took over the old Palmer Shipyard in Noank to build wooden vessels for the cause. Within a year he had secured contracts for twenty-four steel and twelve wooden ships totaling $43 million. Groton and New London residents were jubilant with visions of golden days ahead.

Morse, a business genius known as "Little Napoleon," had already made and lost fortunes in New York, dabbling in the ice market and in steamships lines. He had even served a prison sentence for questionable stock market maneuvers. He was in Groton in September 1917, trying to hurry along construction of the new yard. Some three hundred men and fifteen teams of horses were at work under the direction of O.E. Cutler, general manager.

The launch of the steel freighter *Provincetown* at the Groton Iron Works, the site of today's Pfizer plant, in November 1919 for World War I.

The keel for the first 428-foot steel freighter was laid on January 29, 1918, recorded for the movies by the *Pathe Weekly News*. By this time, 850 men worked at the yard. The force eventually reached 3,500.

Progress was slow. Local reporters were critical; some firms were delivering a vessel a month, but it was not until November 8, 1918, that the first steel vessel, the *Tolland*, entered the cold waters of the Thames. Three days later the armistice was signed, ending the war. In April 1919, the second vessel, the *Worcester*, was launched. Three others followed that year at a total cost of $9.9 million, $1.1 million over contract. Nine ships in all were completed, all too late for war service.

Morse's plans had included a Groton housing project, but the ninety-two dwellings were not finished until April 1919. Most of the workers had to live in New London, some quartered on an old Hudson River steamer anchored near Fort Trumbull. They took the ferry across the river to the shipyard every day.

Unfortunately, the bottom dropped out of the market for Charles S. Morse. Groton Iron Works was consigned to bankruptcy, setting hundreds of workers adrift. In March 1919, the Morse conglomerate, known as the United States Steamship Company, went into receivership.

For months, Morse and his sons, Benjamin, Erwin and Harry, were involved in a struggle with the government over the ironworks. In 1922 they were indicted for conspiracy, but after a long jury trial they were finally acquitted.

The old Groton Iron Works caused many changes to the borough of Groton, now the city. It brought about the building of the four-room Eastern Point School in 1920 to accommodate the population bulge. Memories of the old shipyard remain in street names. Morse Avenue was named for Charles W. Morse, while Cutler Street recalls the yard's superintendent, O.E. Cutler.

THE STORY OF THE ATLANTIC COAST FISHERIES

Atlantic Coast Fisheries, which briefly occupied the old Groton Iron Works site, was a pioneer industry, located between the Thames River and Eastern Point Road. The property had hummed with activity when Charles W. Morse strove to provide steel freighters for the Allies during World War I, but his vessels were all too late to assist in the Kaiser's defeat.

In peacetime the property lay idle until 1927, when Atlantic Coast Fisheries, a New York–based enterprise, purchased part of the thirty-acre tract with an option on the rest. In 1929, it purchased an additional sixteen acres of land, with six buildings plus the concrete shipways and the crane ways. It sold part of this waterfront tract to the Shell Oil Company to become a distributing center for eastern Connecticut. Shell erected three buildings and seven storage tanks and rebuilt an existing trestle, strengthening it for heavy tank cars.

Atlantic Coast Fisheries was an unsung pioneer in the field of frozen foods, specializing in filleting, freezing and packaging haddock. Today we associate Clarence Birdseye with this process. He developed the idea in 1915 on a trip to the Arctic when he discovered that fish, quickly frozen, tasted fresh when thawed. In 1922, he began processing frozen fillets and held many patents in the field. His first efforts to market his products ended in bankruptcy, but he acquired the backing of Postum, later part of General Foods, and went on to great success.

Following this pattern, Atlantic Coast Fisheries established its Groton headquarters in a large waterfront building, once the fitting-out shop for Groton Iron Works. A companion firm, the Portland Trawler Company, had the contract to deliver fresh fish, iced down, to Groton. Its fleet of seventeen vessels traveled off the Georges Banks. Trawlers also served as "carry back" boats, loading fish from other vessels at the fishing grounds for

The Atlantic Coast Fisheries' Groton plant, shown here circa 1930, was a pioneer in the frozen food field, packaging frozen haddock. *Courtesy of Jim Streeter.*

delivery to the plant. Often three or four of these large trawlers tied up at the Groton dock.

Fish from the holds were loaded onto a large conveyor that carried them to noisy filleting and freezing machinery on the second floor of the plant. Another conveyor carried the processed fish to the icy packing room, where girls examined them and packed them in boxes for market. Neighborhood boys congregated to watch as fish was loaded onto the conveyor, and ice was loaded into the holds before trawlers left for the fishing grounds.

In July 1930, the plant was working full force. Trawlers with haddock arrived daily. One fine Monday, trawlers Petrel and Osprey brought in combined catches of 150,000 pounds. Two trawlers were scheduled for the next day with single arrivals expected each day to the end of the week. On July 22, assistant manager James A. Gaynor announced that the plant had hired one hundred women, who were employed in sorting, freezing and packing the fish. Two shifts worked during the afternoon, the second from two until ten o'clock at night. Men were also employed. The 1930 Groton borough directory lists fifty men as employees of Atlantic Coast Fisheries.

A number of Portland trawler employees also made their homes in Groton. The 1930 directory lists George Allison as harbor pilot, John T. Collins and Herbert M. Greene as captains and Garret Linderman as cook. Tomas Cook was chief engineer on one of the boats; his younger brother Hans was cook and deck officer on a trawler.

While it lasted, Atlantic Fisheries was a boon to Groton's economy, but there were problems. Several pounds of haddock were required to produce one pound of fillet, and waste was considerable. The plant had to dispose of unwanted heads, entrails and bones. In the spring of 1930, the company installed $40,000 worth of new machinery to process waste. A similar situation existed for the menhaden industry, which produced fish meal for fertilizer. Menhaden plants were known for their strong odor, and this was true of Atlantic Fisheries when it treated the waste. Two Groton ladies remember the plant only for its disagreeable smell.

The plant went out of business after about five years, due partly to the Great Depression that gripped the land. Its location so far from the fishing grounds added expense to the operation, and the market was not yet ready for frozen products in the 1930s.

The site came back to life in 1942, becoming the Victory Yard. Ten building ways blasted out of solid rock contributed to Electric Boat's record production of seventy-four World War II submarines. The same land today prospers as Pfizer property.

FRANK CABLE BRINGS SUBMARINES TO GROTON

Frank Cable was instrumental in the development of modern submarines, yet when he was offered a chance to take a test run on the *Holland*, the navy's first submarine, he replied, "Not on your life! You couldn't pay me to do that." Fortunately he changed his mind.

Born on his father's farm in Milford, Connecticut, in 1863, he attended Franklin and Drexel Institute in Philadelphia and found a job with the Electro-Dynamic Company in that city as an electrical engineer. This company supplied equipment and motors as well as financing for an ingenious inventor, John Holland, who had developed a submarine that bore his name and which he hoped to sell to the U.S. Navy. On October 13, 1897, the *Holland* sank at its pier when a workman carelessly left the sea valve open.

The vessel was submerged in corrosive saltwater for eighteen hours, to the detriment of the Electro-Dynamic Company's recently installed electrical equipment. The company sent Cable, its star electrical engineer, to repair the damage. He developed an ingenious method to dry out and recondition the wiring and other components. And in spite of Cable's earlier aversion, Holland soon hired him as chief electrician in charge of test operations.

By June 1899, Cable had the title of trial captain and was in charge of the *Holland* until the submarine was turned over to the navy in the fall of 1900. During this time Cable also helped find capital for the new vessel. He interested Isaac L. Rice, president of the Electric Storage Battery Company of Philadelphia. Responding to Cable's enthusiasm, in February 1899 Rice incorporated the Electric Boat Company, which absorbed Holland's Torpedo Boat Company and also the Electric-Dynamic Company, ancestors of our present Electric Boat/General Dynamics firm.

From his successful work as trial captain, Cable developed an international reputation for expertise in submarine matters. He traveled to England to train crews for undersea vessels developed by the Great Britain firm of Vickers. He later went to Japan and Russia to assist in training submarine crews.

Finding suitable engines to propel these new submarines was a constant challenge. Early gasoline engines were far from satisfactory. In Germany, Dr. Rudolf Diesel had invented the diesel engine in 1892. The Electric Boat Company was quick to realize the possibilities of this new invention. Through contacts with the Vickers firm, Electric Boat secured a license

Frank Cable, shown in a contemporary cartoon, helped establish the New London Ship and Engine Company, predecessor of General Dynamics. *Courtesy of United States Submarines.*

to build twelve of the new engines. Its subsidiary, Fore River shipyard at Quincy, Massachusetts, was selected for the job.

When the Fore River shipyard proved unequal to the task, the Electric Boat Company decided to establish a new plant for that purpose and assigned Captain Cable the job of finding a suitable site. The captain located the ideal spot in Groton on the east bank of the Thames River, where the Eastern Shipbuilding Company had constructed the mammoth ocean liners *Minnesota* and *Dakota* at the turn of the century. Prior to that, the Shoreline railroad ferry had occupied the same location.

At this point Electric Boat organized a new subsidiary, the New London Ship and Engine Company, known locally as NELSECO, with Lawrence Y. Spear as president and Cable as vice president and general manager. It leased the property from the railroad for $5,000 per year. Cable signed the lease for NELSECO, providing that the premises were to be used

> *for the purpose of building boats and vessels of every kind, manufacturing and constructing appliances and machinery in general, building engines for marine and other purposes and manufacturing torpedoes and all machinery and appliances used in construction therewith.*

Work on the site began in 1910 and was completed the following year. The company leased machinery for the machine shop from a New Jersey firm, Niles-Bemont-Pond Company, including a traveling crane. Money was tight, and Cable and the technical department employees had to raise funds on their own. To begin with, the diesel engines started at Quincy were completed in Groton, the first marine diesels built in America. In 1917, the *Skipjack E-1*, powered with a diesel, became the first American submarine to cross the Atlantic Ocean.

During World War I, NELSECO built diesels, submarine parts and gasoline engines for subchasers. There was no shipyard until 1922, when one was needed to overhaul S-class submarines. Then the company decided to do its own shipbuilding and expanded the Groton facilities. In 1925, the first submarine was built there, not for the U.S. Navy but for Peru. The company's first contract to build a United States submarine came in 1931, resulting in the *Cuttlefish*, the first submarine to have a welded hull. When NELSECO merged with the Electric Boat Company in 1930, Cable was promoted to general manager of the firm.

Frank Cable died on May 21, 1945. The man who had refused a trip on the *Holland* did very well for himself and his country, devoting his life to the world of submarines.

L.Y. SPEAR

A Life in Submarines

Lawrence Y. Spear, well remembered in these parts, was "the grand old man of submarines" according to Vice Admiral Charles A. Lockwood. Altogether, Spear devoted forty-eight years of his life to submarine construction. He was a judge's son born in 1870 in Warren, Ohio, a good distance from the sea, but this Midwesterner had a tremendous influence on the development of undersea craft.

Entering Annapolis at the age of sixteen, he graduated second in his class. The navy sent the promising ensign to study marine engineering at the University of Glasgow in Scotland. When he returned with his degree, he taught naval architecture to postgraduate students at the U.S.

Submarine *R-2* passes the Groton Monument about 1926, en route to the U.S. Naval Submarine Base upstream.

Naval Academy. Later he was assistant superintendent of construction for Admiral Dewey's famous flagship, *Olympia*. But at the turn of the century, the direction of his life changed.

Now a young lieutenant, his tour of duty took him to the Crescent Shipyard of the Electric Boat Company, where John Holland's early submarines were undergoing testing for the navy. Spear watched the submarine *Fulton* set a record of fifteen hours for submersion. He was so impressed that he renounced his promising naval career, resigned his commission in 1902 and took a job with the infant Electric Boat Company. He soon became vice president, responsible for submarine design and construction, working with John Holland, the inventor, and Frank Cable, head of the test crew, and charged with developing the navy's first submarine fleet.

Holland was a man of ideas, but was not always practical as to how they could be carried out. He resented Spear and Cable, who shied way from Holland's Jules Verne and Rube Goldberg approach, preferring the nuts and bolts of practical, workable construction to visionary plans of the inventor. After one skirmish over steering mechanism, Holland called Spear "a young whippersnapper from the navy," complaining that Spear would ruin his life's work.

Quite the contrary. From the start Spear realized the potential of the submarine. In 1906, in a paper delivered to the Society of Naval Architects, he predicted the growth in the size and capabilities of the underwater fleet, emphasizing qualities of submerged speed, surface speed and strength and hull safety. He is credited with implementing the basic design concepts of modern seagoing submarines, including double-hull amidships, single-hull ends and propelling apparatus.

In 1911, Electric Boat sent Frank Cable to Groton to establish the New London Ship and Engine Company, known as NELSECO, a plant to produce diesel engines for the submarines it was constructing. L.Y. Spear became president of the firm. His interest was always in submarines, and as early as 1915 he was advocating their use in coastal defense and stressing their importance as an offensive weapon in enemy waters.

Following World War I, the parent Electric Boat Company fell on lean times, with no U.S. Navy submarine contracts for thirteen years. Thanks to Spear's ingenuity, NELSECO managed to keep going. He secured contracts for four subs for Peru and for various vessels for other foreign countries, keeping the firm in business.

On December 17, 1927, the submarine *S-4* went to the bottom off Provincetown after a collision with a Coast Guard destroyer. Spear came out strongly for the development of a means of escape in case of disaster, saying what was needed was a watertight rescue chamber to bring trapped men to the surface. Eventually the navy perfected the McCann Rescue Chamber, used with success at the *Squalus* disaster.

In 1929, the Groton plant officially became the NELSECO Division of the Electric Boat Company, with L.Y. Spear as vice president and general manager and Frank Cable as business manager. In 1931, they secured a contract for the U.S. Navy. The USS *Cuttlefish* was launched two years later, the first submarine with a welded hull.

Advocating designs that optimized surface performance and ocean cruising, as well as undersea performance, Spear continued his important role in building the submarines that defended America after Pearl Harbor. He was named president of Electric Boat in 1942. The advent of World War II had proved the accuracy of his vision. Electric Boat delivered seventy-four of the famous fleet-type submarines to the navy, more than any yard in America. Groton-built submarines accounted for 39 percent of all Japanese shipping destroyed in the Pacific.

When the Groton yard became the Electric Boat Division of General Dynamics in 1947, Spear became chairman of the board, a position he held for three years until his death in Groton on September 9, 1950. In his honor, the tender USS *L.Y. Spear* (AS 36) was launched at Quincy, Massachusetts, in 1967, fittingly built by General Dynamics. The 643-foot vessel was the first ship designed to service nuclear attack submarines and was capable of tending up to four subs moored alongside simultaneously. The USS *L.Y. Spear* was decommissioned in 1999, but the man it honored holds his place in history.

GROTON SEA CAPTAINS

SISSON'S LEGENDARY CROSSING

Captain James W. Sisson became a hero during the fierce winter storm that began on February 26, 1886. His miraculous escape is part of Groton's folklore. That night the thermometer registered five degrees Fahrenheit, it was snowing and the raw northwest wind reached a velocity of sixty miles per hour. Through angry waves and mountainous seas, Captain Sisson somehow made his way in a small dory across the stormy waters of the sound to Fishers Island and lived to tell his tale.

Sisson was employed as mate on the *Annie D.*, a makeshift light boat for Stonington Line steamers. The old fishing smack was anchored near Ram Island, where an unmarked reef provided a serious menace to navigation as it lay in the route of the giant floating palaces. To prevent disaster, the steamboat company maintained the *Annie D.* in seven fathoms of water just south of the reef. With lighted lanterns high on the mast, the smack guided the majestic side-wheelers past the danger.

When the storm broke that night, Sisson was alone on the forty-seven-foot light boat. His usual companion, Captain N.B. Vars, was ashore. Sisson, who lived in Westerly, was an experienced seaman with one sealing voyage to the Antarctic to his credit, and he was not afraid of bad weather.

The twenty-three-ton *Annie D.* bobbed around like a cork in the storm, but the acting keeper knew the vessel was sturdy. The craft was built in 1859 by Noank master builder Deacon Robert Palmer for Captain Ezra Daboll, who named the boat for his daughter. The deacon still owned one-eighth interest in the *Annie D.*

Captain Sisson soon decided this was no ordinary blow. By 11:00 p.m. huge seas were breaking over the *Annie D.*, filling its deck with water. Sisson grabbed a maul and knocked a few boards from the bulwarks so the water ran off, but the thumping of the waves started the seams leaking. In bitter cold, the water froze and ice formed forward, pulling the vessel's bow low in the water.

Sisson went below to warm up in the cabin, but the fire was out. By midnight, water was coming in. He decided to go back on deck. He knew he would have to fight for his life. He removed all of his heavy woolen

Deacon Palmer's shipyard in Noank, where the smack *Annie D.* was built in 1859.

outer garments and went up on deck wearing only an undershirt and drawers beneath his oilskins. He figured heavy clothes would only freeze stiff and keep him from moving freely.

On deck he worked like a demon to keep the *Annie D.* afloat, but he saw that the craft was doomed. His one chance to escape was to use the smack's dory, but it was filled with water and frozen fast to the deck. He grabbed his axe and tried to chop it free, but as fast as he loosened one spot, it froze in another. It was an uncomfortable Friday night.

When Saturday dawned cold and gray, Deacon Palmer looked out from the cupola of his handsome house in Noank. Amid whitecaps on the sound, he saw the *Annie D.* flying a distress signal. (The deacon's house still stands high on Palmer Court, once nicknamed Noank's haunted house.)

Through binoculars, the deacon watched Sisson's efforts. He thought the *Annie D.* was lost along with his investment. No Noank craft was large enough to put out in such a storm, but Palmer telegraphed to New London for a rescue vessel. It came too late.

At 9:15 a.m., the *Annie D.*'s bowsprit went under, and Sisson thought it was the end. A huge sea swept over the deck, leaving the smack low in the water. But the wave filled the dory and wrenched it free, and the dory began to move.

The next sea set the dory adrift. Sisson managed to jump in amidships and floated away. He had traveled just three boat lengths away when the *Annie D.* went to the bottom.

It was all the captain could do to balance the dory, which was full of water and ice. He sat in the bottom and bailed when he could. He could not see to steer. His hat was covered with ice. Icicles covered his face and beard. He couldn't move his fingers until he soaked his mitten in the frigid water to thaw the ice. There was nothing he could do but crouch low and try to stay alive.

Sisson figured the wind would sweep him toward Fishers Island, and there was a bare chance he could reach the shore. When he heard seas breaking, he took up his oars and pulled with all his strength. He finally landed the dory near Money Pond and climbed painfully up on the bank.

Numb with cold, his wet clothes a moving mass of ice, he managed to reach a farmhouse before he collapsed. The family rescued and revived him.

From the cupola in Noank, the deacon and his friends watched Sisson's wild journey, but had no way of knowing whether he had reached shelter or had died of exposure on the shore. Early Sunday morning, when the storm had diminished, the steamer *Eva*, with a volunteer crew, left Noank for Fishers Island, taking Dr. Orrin E. Miner for medical aid.

The *Eva* returned to Noank at 1:00 p.m. A large crowd waiting at the wharf cheered when James W. Sisson stepped ashore, still shaky, with one ear and one finger frozen, but miraculously alive.

Two weeks later, when the steamboat company engaged the sloop *Napoleon* as a lightship, Captain Sisson was ready to take up his duty on the new vessel.

Of such stuff heroes are made.

HENRY DAVIS AND CLEOPATRA'S NEEDLE

Captain Henry E. Davis was a Groton mariner, but his career was far from typical. He was born near Old Mystic on September 20, 1826, but he claimed Noank as his home for most of his life. In his early years, he shipped aboard Noank fishing smacks. Later he turned to shipbuilding and learned the trade at Noank's famous Palmer Shipyard. He eventually deserted the sea altogether for building and construction ashore.

He tackled his most famous project in 1869, the stone structure of the second Noank lighthouse at Morgan Point, which still exists today although

Cleopatra's Needle, an Egyptian obelisk in Central Park, New York City, was brought to America with the construction genius of Captain Henry Davis of Noank.

the original building has been much changed and enlarged. His Noank masterpiece was probably the huge Victorian home built for Deacon Palmer, his former boss at the shipyard. This lofty mansion is one of Noank's most picturesque, and it is easy to picture the old deacon watching the sea from the tower that caps this imposing structure.

Henry Davis is remembered for more than his houses. In 1879, he was chosen for a special government task. Egypt's ancient civilization was headline news at the time, and the United States wanted an Egyptian relic to display. Great Britain boasted an obelisk obtained in 1878, and negotiations were under way to obtain a similar monument from the khedive of Egypt to exhibit in New York.

The khedive agreed to export an obelisk of rose red granite dating to 1500 BC, an object quickly dubbed "Cleopatra's Needle," although that famous beauty had nothing whatever to do with it. This impressive stone shaft measured sixty-nine feet and six inches long and weighed 224 tons. It had been transported from its inland site to the Alexandria waterfront, and now the government chose Henry Davis to oversee its journey across the ocean to New York.

Davis left Noank on August 25, 1879. He faced a Herculean task. The expedition was led by Lieutenant Commodore Henry Honychurch Gorringe, United States Navy, but Davis was in charge of building the launching ways and pontoons, excavating for piers and locating or constructing derricks to move the obelisk. They needed a vessel capable of carrying the needle across the Atlantic. Gorringe finally found the steamer *Dessoug*, which he purchased from the Egyptian government.

Davis adapted the ship to accommodate the obelisk and the pedestal stone. He also supervised the complicated work of loading Cleopatra's Needle into the *Dessoug*.

They sailed from Alexandria on June 12, 1880, safely weathering the stormy Atlantic—a tribute to Davis's skill. This was a record-breaking voyage, as the obelisk was the heaviest single object ever transported in an oceangoing ship of the time. They anchored in New York on July 20, and Davis's work was done; he went home to Noank.

Later the needle passed slowly through the streets of New York, drawn by sixteen pairs of horses. It reached Central Park 112 days later, a distance of 2.1 miles, moving ninety-nine feet per day. It was swung into place behind the Metropolitan Museum of Art on January 22, 1881, where it may still be seen, one of only thirty Egyptian obelisks remaining in the world. It is now somewhat eroded by the elements.

Henry Davis entered another form of government service on August 18, 1885, becoming assistant superintendent of construction for lifesaving stations on the Atlantic and Pacific Coasts. In 1896, returning to an earlier scene, he built an innovative floating lifesaving station at the Palmer Shipyard. In 1903, at the age of seventy-eight, he supervised the construction of another station at East Harbor, Fishers Island.

Groton boasts dozens of mariners, but Captain Henry Davis was not your average sea captain. He has left us many tangible evidences of his talent. He died in Noank in 1909, but his works endure.

WILLIAM H. APPELMAN

A Colorful Career

If you are thinking that life at sea would be exciting, consider the career of Groton captain William H. Appelman, a resident of Mystic Village. A successful fisherman, he survived the loss of his smack off Jupiter Inlet in a gale and made three successful sealing voyages in the Antarctic before he finally disappeared in the cold South Polar seas.

He was one of the eight sons of a Swedish captain, John Appelman, who came to Mystic before the War of 1812. John built a house on Gravel

Street and soon became a leader in the maritime village. Most of his sons went to sea, except for Hiram, who distinguished himself as a colonel in the Civil War and later became Connecticut's secretary of state.

Like his father, William fished in southern waters. In the fall he sailed his forty-four-foot smack to Key West to fish through the winter, selling his catch in Havana. In 1865, he rejoiced in the ownership of a new twenty-five-ton smack, *Minnie*, but not for long. On October 25 his vessel foundered in a Florida gale. The captain, his son Willie, Sanford Stark and two others of the crew were picked up by the steamer *F.L. Fung Chung* and deposited in New York. The $4,500 *Minnie* was not insured. In the same gale, William's brother Erastus went missing on the smack *Connecticut* with all his crew.

Undeterred from a life at sea, the next year William had the thirty-ton sloop *Nevada* built at New London. Sailing out of Key West he made three unusual fishing trips, collecting specimens for showman P.T. Barnum. He brought the fish back alive to New York to be exhibited in the aquarium of Barnum's famous museum.

He returned to less exotic fishing in the sloop *Alaska*. He was back in Mystic in May 1869, after a six-day passage from Havana, reporting that fishing was dull because of the threat of war in Spain. In June 1870, he once more arrived in Mystic from Havana. Business was so bad that he had tried to bring home a cargo of pineapples to sell, but

The Straits of Magellan. Groton native Captain William Appelman was lost on a sealing voyage to the Antarctic.

they spoiled quickly and he was obliged to put in at Wilmington, North Carolina, to dispose of them. There was still no favorable report from Havana. When business finally improved, he and his partners from Key West had a new sixty-ton smack, *Florida*, built by the Mystic firm of Hill & Grinnell. He spent the winter of 1872 "salt fishing," catching and curing mullet in Charlotte's harbor and selling the salted fish in Havana. He took over five loads and made a good profit.

Returning home, he decided to try his luck at the more profitable but also more dangerous business of sealing, sealskins being much in demand for winter clothing at the time. As master of the Stonington schooner *Thomas Hunt*, sixty-three tons, he sailed for the Antarctic. While he was away in the summer of 1873, his wife Lois opened a gift shop in her home on Appelman Point at the head of Gravel Street, where she sold framed pictures and other novelties.

William made three profitable sealing voyages in thirty months and lost neither man nor boat. He brought the *Thomas Hunt* home in April 1876 with 680 South Shetland skins and 200 furs from South Georgia. With skins scarce and the prices high, the cargo was valued at $30,000. This success earned him the command of a larger vessel, the ninety-seven-ton *Charles Shearer*, also out of Stonington. He sailed in July, taking as his first mate his son, William H. Appelman Jr.

In April 1877, the *Mystic Press* reported that the *Shearer* was at the Shetland Islands with 431 skins, and in August it claimed that Appelman was at Fayal, where he had taken two whales yielding thirty barrels of oil. After that there was only silence. The village became anxious about the *Charles Shearer*. In May, residents learned that a British ship had picked up six men from the *Shearer* crew. Appelman had left them sealing on the Diego Ramirez Islands off Cape Horn. They were glad to be rescued. The captain was a month overdue and they were short of provisions.

Alone and worried about her husband and son, Lois Appelman appealed to the secretary of the navy, requesting that he send vessels to search for the *Shearer*. Her appeal was backed by letters from the governor of Connecticut. But the only navy ships in the South Atlantic were the *Hartford* and the *Essex*, both too large to enter inlets and bays where the schooner might be caught in the ice. Months passed, and in April 1879, two years after the *Shearer* sailed, the captain's former command, the *Thomas Hunt*, arrived in Stonington, bringing the fifteen hundred skins left by the *Shearer*'s crew on the Diegos. There was no news of the Appelmans, father and son.

At a Groton probate court on June 5, 1879, Mrs. Lois N. Appelman was appointed administrator of her husband's estate. When affairs were settled, there was a balance of $33.16, not much to show for a life at sea. And to this day, no one knows what happened to William H. Appelman and his men in the cruel southern ocean.

RATTLER MORGAN

Groton Whaling Captain

Captain Ebenezer "Rattler" Morgan was one of the area's most successful maritime captains, amassing a fortune of close to $1 million before he died. His Groton home on Monument Street still exists and is presently under restoration, a significant historic property.

Ebenezer Morgan, born in Groton on July 22, 1817, was orphaned at an early age and went to sea as a cabin boy when he was only ten, an age when most boys today are entering the fifth grade. He followed the sea for forty-one years, setting many records in his time. He was described as a competent, short, stocky man with a nicely trimmed beard and energetic in both action and speech. It is not clear why he was nicknamed "Rattler." Some think it was because he spoke so rapidly, rattling off his words; another view is that he had a rattling good time in life.

Rattler was born when it was possible for a smart lad to go to sea and make a fortune, rising rapidly through the ranks. By the age of thirty he commanded the whale ship *Julius Caesar*, 346 tons, a profitable vessel whose agent was E.V. Stoddard. On his third voyage in this vessel, he spent months in the Indian Ocean at Desolation Island. Nathaniel W. Taylor, on board as medical officer, wrote a detailed account of this voyage that was published by the New London County Historical Society as *Life on Whaler*, a wonderful book that is still available. Taylor relates that Morgan brought his twenty-three-year-old wife Ann along on this voyage, fitting up a cozy cabin for her. "She was the mother of a boy two years old whom she had left at home with his grandparents. She was the perfect picture of good health and good humor and was endowed with an uncommon degree of courage," Taylor wrote.

Rattler's early whaling voyages were successful but routine. However, in 1864, in the sailing bark *Pioneer*, he made what has been called the greatest voyage on record. The ship's owners, Williams & Haven, had invested $35,800 in the vessel. He was gone only fifteen months, and upon his return the cargo sold for $151,060, a profit of more than 400 percent on the investment. Part of Rattler's share went to the construction of his Italianate villa on Monument Street.

Figuring the *Pioneer* a lucky vessel, Rattler and its owners tried a novel experiment. They converted the *Pioneer* into a steamship, adding an engine, and sent it north under Rattler. Although the voyage was not impressive for its profitable cargo, it is notable because this was the first steam whaler outfitted in the United States.

Next, about to set another first, Rattler left whaling and turned to sealing. Aware that Secretary Seward was negotiating the purchase of Alaska for the United States, Rattler's firm outfitted the bark *Peru* and sent the captain hurrying north. There, arriving at St. Paul's Island in the Pribilofs, Morgan raised the first American flag on Alaskan soil. In the face of stiff competition, he managed to come away with forty-five thousand sealskins and a longtime monopoly. Back in New London, this led to the formation of the Alaska Commercial Company, with the officers of Williams & Haven as stockholders along with Rattler Morgan. The wily captain had negotiated a twenty-year exclusive lease of the seal rookeries that would not expire until 1890. Wealth poured into New London and Groton as a result of his work.

That was Rattler's last voyage. He retired from the sea and settled down to enjoy his ornate Groton residence. In retirement, Rattler established a reputation for philanthropy, donating sizeable sums to churches and charities. He was one of the pillars of the Groton Heights Baptist Church, located not far from his home. His hobby was presenting stacks of Bibles to the crews of vessels leaving the port of New London. According to the *Mystic Press*, on one occasion in 1883, armed with volumes for the schooner *Francis Allyn*, he arrived too late. The vessel had already left the wharf. Rattler chartered the steamer *Niantic*, overtook the *Allyn* and presented his gift to the crew.

He also invested widely in property at Groton Bank. Several houses that he built are still standing. A house at 115 Broad Street was probably his first home. Wealthy and successful, he died on August 11, 1890, at the age of seventy-three. Legends of Rattler have become part of Groton's heritage.

THE RESOLUTE DESK IN THE OVAL OFFICE

Its Groton Links

In *Time* magazine, the issue for September 6, 2004, I found a picture of President George W. Bush in the Oval Office. The issue was titled, "The World According to George Bush," so that was not surprising. But what really startled me was that our president is shown lounging back in his chair with his loafer-clad feet resting on the elegantly carved Resolute desk that has been a feature of that office for most presidential terms since 1880.

Barbara Bush always seemed a pleasant and sensible lady. I'm sure she didn't raise her boy to put his feet on the furniture, especially a historic piece like the Resolute desk. And especially not with his shoes on. That desk has a story. It involves our part of the country and a Groton whaling captain named James Monroe Buddington.

The Resolute desk, now in the Oval Office of the White House, was made from timbers of a ship rescued in the Arctic by Groton's Captain James Monroe Buddington.

Captain Buddington in later years with his second wife.

I've written about Captain Buddington before, but a good story deserves retelling, and there may be people who do not know how that desk came to be in the White House. James Monroe Buddington was a whaling captain, born on a farm in Center Groton in 1817. He hated farming, and after his fourteenth birthday he snuck away and signed on as cabin boy on a New London whaler. Seven years later he commanded a whaler himself, specializing in Arctic whaling.

In May 1855, Buddington sailed from New London in the bark *George Henry* with a crew of twenty-five to hunt whales in the Arctic near Davis Strait. Whales were scarce that year, and they encountered large ice fields where the bark forced its way through dangerous floes. On September 10, near Cape Mercy, the captain saw in the distance an abandoned vessel frozen fast in the ice.

He sent four men to examine the derelict. They returned with the news that it was the HMS *Resolute*, abandoned by its captain in the Arctic in 1854 after a fruitless search for a missing British explorer, Sir John Franklin. Its crew had secured the hatches and left it, taking only their navigation instruments. The sturdy ship, built of teakwood timbers, had survived sixteen months of drifting in the Polar seas.

Buddington figured it would be more profitable to rescue the British ship than to look for whales. He went aboard with ten men and the ship's carpenter, rigged the sails as best he could and, with difficulty, sailed the *Resolute* to New London. He had no chronometer and no charts or maps, but with only his watch, a quadrant and a miserable compass he managed the long voyage home. He arrived triumphantly in the harbor on a frigid Christmas Day. Crowds crossed the frozen Thames, thronging to inspect the vessel and hear the tale of its rescue.

In 1856, Senator James M. Mason proposed that the United States buy the *Resolute*, refit it properly and send it back to England. Accordingly, the ship was purchased from the *George Henry*'s owners for $40,000 and restored by the government as a gift for Queen Victoria and a token of friendship. The work was done at the Brooklyn Navy Yard. The ship sailed for England in perfect condition on November 13, 1856, and the queen herself trod the decks in December, graciously accepting this symbol of alliance.

When the HMS *Resolute* was outdated and scrapped in 1879, Queen Victoria ordered that three desks be made from the deck timbers. One was given to Mrs. Henry Grinnell, whose husband had supported the Franklin search. The second was sent to Captain Buddington himself. The third went to Washington, D.C., in 1880, presented as a token of appreciation to Rutherford B. Hayes, then president of our country. Beautifully carved and bearing a plaque relating its history, the desk has been used by every president since Hayes, with the exceptions of Lyndon B. Johnson, Richard M. Nixon and Gerald R. Ford. In the happy days of John F. Kennedy's presidency, young John Kennedy Jr. loved to hide beneath it in games with his father. A replica of the desk was made later for Jacqueline Kennedy Onassis for display at the Kennedy Memorial in Massachusetts.

James Monroe Buddington returned to the business of whaling, but the glory days had passed. Once, he even left the sea to try his hand at farming, but he eventually went back to command the schooner *Era* on an Arctic expedition. He died in Sailor's Snug Harbor in 1908. No one knows what happened to his Resolute desk.

Fortunately, the presidential Resolute desk is still in the Oval Office, even though Barbara Bush's son sometimes uses it for a footstool. That's a tough desk made of enduring teak, and I suppose it won't do much harm if he does put his feet on it. Personally, I think that historic piece of furniture deserves better treatment.

CAPTAIN SPICER AND THE ESKIMOS

After December snows I think of the Polar regions, which bring to mind the story of the Eskimo John Bull, who made a great impression when he visited Groton and New London in 1881. Captain John O. Spicer, a leading whaling master, brought him from the Arctic to testify in a lawsuit. Along with John Bull came his wife, Annie Kimilu, and their little daughter, Kudlarjuk. The trio posed for their picture at the Bishop Studios in New London, an image now carefully preserved in the collections of New London County Historical Society.

John Bull's real name was Johnibo, but American whalers were fond of supplying the natives with nicknames that were easier to pronounce and remember. He first became acquainted with Captain Spicer about 1877, when Spicer was exploring along the north coast of the Hudson Strait near Baffin Land and chanced upon an area in which the Eskimos said there were always whales.

Captain John O. Spicer, leading Groton whaling captain and expert on Arctic whaling. *Courtesy of the Spicer family.*

Eskimos John Bull, Annie Kimilu and their daughter Kedlarjuk came to Groton in 1881 so John Bull could testify in a lawsuit.

Spicer had spent much time whaling the Arctic. He had even lived there for forty-four months in a whaling station he had built on the Cumberland Gulf, gathering whale oil and ferrying it back to New London in various vessels. He was well acquainted with Inuit culture. He liked the natives and was respected by them. Early on he became acquainted with John Bull, who was a well-known "whaling boss" noted for assisting American whale men.

In July 1879, Spicer noted in the log of his vessel, the *Era*, that he "engaged John Bull and his crew to go to Hudson Strait to whale." The *Era* sailed off after outfitting John Bull and his men, leaving them to work through the summer capturing whales. The products of their labor were picked up later. This was the beginning of a successful association with John Bull.

In the following spring, Captain Spicer again deployed John Bull and two boat crews in the Hudson Strait. They successfully captured three whales, but this time Spicer and the *Era* were late in returning. When the Groton captain finally came, the bone, oil and blubber had disappeared, taken away by rival American whalers. Two New Bedford whalers had convinced John Bull that Spicer's vessel had foundered and that he was not coming back. In spite of the Inuit's protests, they confiscated the whale products without his permission and sailed away.

By astute detective work and by questioning the natives, Captain Spicer learned that the guilty vessels were the *Abbie Bradford* and the *George and Mary* of New Bedford. He interviewed John Bull and paid him a whaleboat for his trouble, took statements from other witnesses and sailed for home. He reached New London on November 24, 1880, furious at his loss. At once he traveled to New Bedford, accosted the captains and owners responsible for the theft and demanded restitution. "It is your privilege to go to the courts," they told him.

Spicer worked for the whaling firm of C.A. Williams & Company, and they gave him full backing. They hired the best lawyers, and Spicer sent for John Bull and family to come to Groton to serve as his witness.

The case attracted wide attention when it opened on June 6, 1882, in Boston. The defense claimed that Eskimos were not of sufficient intelligence to make contracts or to testify in court, but Captain Spicer put his faith in John Bull, who was a very satisfactory witness. Through an interpreter he testified for Spicer, giving vital evidence in the case. "No witness made a better impression on the court," a reporter noted. So John O. Spicer won his case and received a satisfactory financial settlement plus damages.

John Bull, Kimilu and the five-year-old Kudlarjuk had been living in Groton with the Spicer family. When the case was over, the captain tried to persuade his star witness to make Groton his home. He found a house for him and bought him a dog, a gun and a boat. He took him to New London on the ferry and to the barbershop. But John Bull hated our climate and longed to go home. At last he convinced Captain Spicer to arrange his return to the north on a whaler out of New London. Just before they sailed, a daughter was born to Kimilu. They called the baby American Girl.

It would be nice to report that the story had a happy ending. Spicer received his money, John Bull proved that Eskimos could testify in court and in the end the Inuit family went back north where they wanted to be.

However, in 1889 the periodical *Whalemen's Shipping List and Merchants' Transcript* reported that John Bull had been murdered. "John Bull was killed over a quarrel about the whalers," said his relatives. Though the reasons are not clear, it may be that people feared him because he had lived in the States and had acquired too much knowledge. "He knew too much," said his daughter Kudlarjuk.

A full account of the trial, called "The Case of the Missing Whales," may be found in Dorothy Eber's book, *When the Whalers Were Up North*.

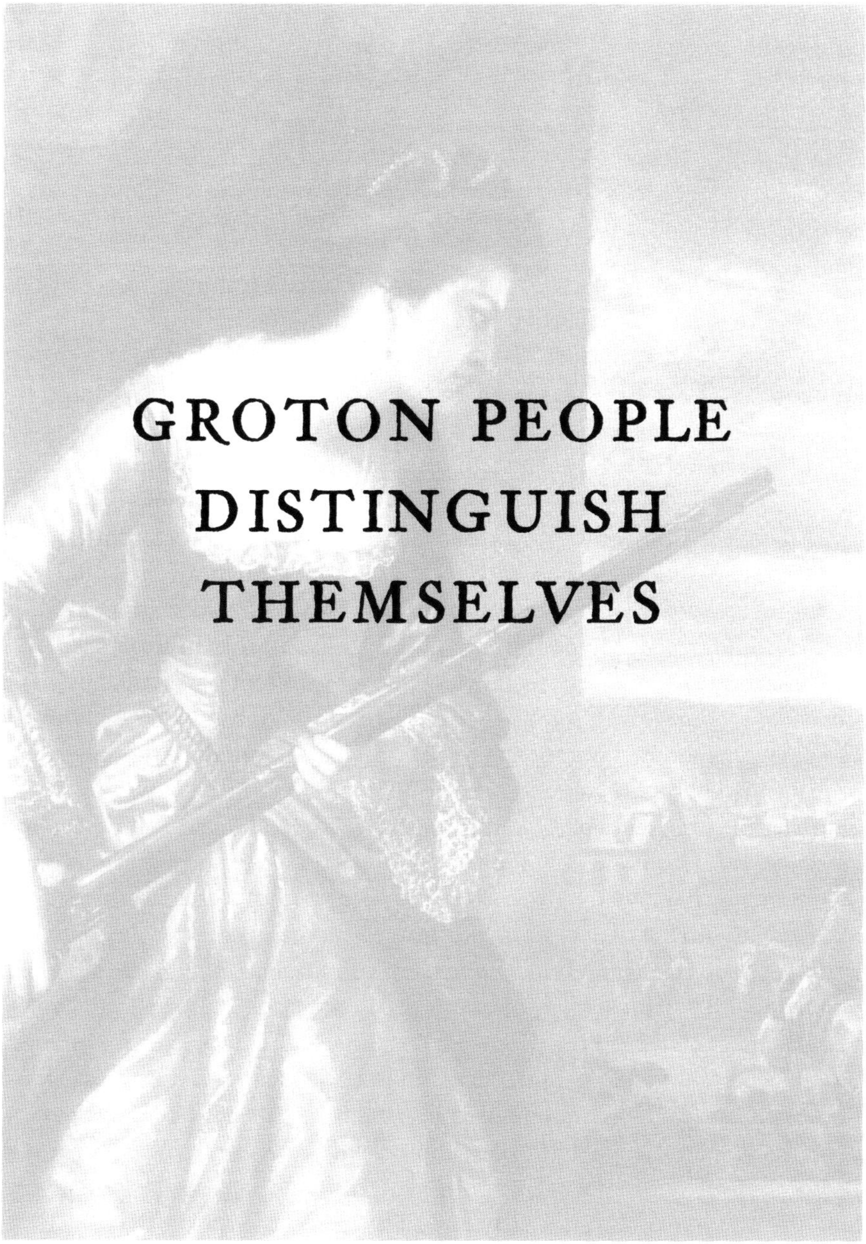

GROTON PEOPLE DISTINGUISH THEMSELVES

ASA PACKER

A Groton Native Who Made Good

You don't hear much about Asa Packer these days, but he was one Groton native who surely made good. He left his Mystic home in 1822 when he was seventeen, with only the clothes on his back, to walk several hundred long miles to his cousin's home in Susquehanna County, Pennsylvania. By sheer hard work and ingenuity, in the good old-fashioned way, he became the third wealthiest man in the United States by 1852, worth an estimated $331 million dollars.

Packer made his money in canals, railroads and the coal trade, and along the way founded Lehigh University. He was into politics too. He ran for governor of Pennsylvania and once was mentioned as a candidate for the presidency of the United Sates. He was unsuccessful in these bids, but in everything else his life was the great American success story.

He was one of four children of Elisha and Desire Packer, born on December 29, 1805, in the small red cottage that still stands on New London Road in Mystic, just across from the late, lamented Mystic Ice House, on what the natives call Ice House Curve. Most Mystic lads went to sea, and many Packers were sea captains, but Asa took the overland route to his cousin's, where he apprenticed as a carpenter. For some years it seemed the wrong choice. He couldn't find work at this trade, and after his marriage to Sarah Blakeslee in 1828 he turned to farming, but they were as poor as church mice.

Looking for better prospects, Asa traveled to Mauch Chunk, Pennsylvania, in the winter of 1832 to captain a canalboat on the Lehigh canal. He moved his family there the next summer and was on his way to success and good fortune. His carpenter training did not go amiss, for he took a contract for building additional canal locks on the upper Lehigh River, an act that proved very successful. Branching out, his brother Robert joined him and together they constructed boats on the Schuylkill River to carry coal to New York. Industrial demand made this very profitable and soon he was a wealthy man.

Asa had a knack for seeing future needs. Canalboats couldn't run in the winter when canals were frozen, stopping coal traffic. Asa turned to rail transportation. He risked most of his capital in 1851 to purchase the stock of

Asa Packer, a Groton native who established Lehigh University in Pennsylvania.

an unfinished railroad, and a year later he completed the road and connected it to others running to New York and Philadelphia, laying the framework for the Lehigh Valley Railroad. By this time he was rolling in money.

The Packers had scrimped in the first years of their marriage, but now Asa could splurge. He had a fine mansion built at Mauch Chunk, a town that has been renamed Jim Thorpe, Pennsylvania. The couple moved in on October 16, 1861. The Italianate villa has eighteen rooms, topped by a cupola, built to last with a cast-iron frame. Designed by architect Samuel Sloan of Philadelphia, it cost $14,000. Years later, in 1878, when Asa and Sarah celebrated their golden wedding anniversary, they renovated the home at a cost of $85,000 and held a housewarming in which they entertained fifteen hundred guests.

Feeling the need to provide the nation with enlightened leadership, Asa established Lehigh College in Bethlehem in 1865 to offer a well-rounded education for youths, something he himself had not enjoyed. He endowed the institution with fifty-six acres of land and $500,000 in railroad stock. Some alumni requested that it be made solely an engineering school, but Asa insisted that literature and history were essential. Today, Lehigh has an undergraduate body of more than forty-five hundred, with two thousand graduate students.

Asa was a religious man. He made sure that every Lehigh student attended chapel. But he was kept out of the local Presbyterian Church because he refused to sign a temperance pledge. When he learned that the nearby Episcopal Church consented to an occasional glass of wine, he transferred his membership to St. Mark's.

Asa Packer died on May 17, 1879, leaving an estate valued at over $54 million, estimated at about $3.2 billion in today's values. In 1912 his daughter, Mary Packer Cummings, willed the family house and all its contents to the Borough of Mauch Chunk as a memorial to her father and his life's work. The mansion remained closed for many years. However, the Jim Thorpe Lions were named trustees in 1954, and the Asa Packer Mansion Museum opened to the public two years later. Designated a National Historic Landmark in 1985, it is regularly opened to the public.

THE STORY OF HALEY FARM STATE PARK

"Write a column about Haley Farm," my friend Nicky suggested during our morning exercise class. As usual she was wearing her blue cardigan. She removes it only when our trainer Jeremy is really merciless. She likes to walk at the farm and was curious about its origins.

Groton's Haley Farm, 264 acres of green space preserved under the Department of Environmental Protection of the State of Connecticut, is one of the town's attractions. Its rolling pastures, stone walls and freshwater ponds remind us of quiet, serene days when this was an agricultural community. Located beside Palmer's Cover, north of Groton Long Point, Haley Farm is popular with hikers, runners and bicyclists, as well as those who love to stroll with their dogs.

We're lucky to have this fine spot for public enjoyment. In the 1960s it was up for residential development, but the Groton Open Space Association, headed by Charles and Priscilla Pratt, raised more than $50,000 toward its purchase for parkland and the town has benefited ever since.

Caleb Haley, shown in his New York office, developed a model farm that is now part of Groton's open spaces. *Courtesy of Priscilla Wright Pratt.*

This prime property was once owned by John Winthrop Jr., founder of the original Pequot Plantation of which the present town of Groton was a part. Known as the eastern neck, or Fort Hill farm, it was rented out until 1789, when the Winthrop heirs sold it to Starr Chester. A small, ancient cemetery with Chester family gravestones still remains. Eventually, it was acquired and developed into a model farm by Groton native Caleb Haley, who had made his fortune in the Fulton Fish Market in New York in the approved Horatio Alger tradition.

Caleb was born at Center Groton on July 27, 1838, the son of Colonel Nelson Haley and his wife Cordelia. After a brief stint working in the local office of Charles Mallory, when he was not yet seventeen Caleb left his father's fields and went to New York to enter the business world. Starting out as bookkeeper for his uncle Dudley Haley in the Fulton Fish Market, he was destined for success. His marriage to Elizabeth Miller, daughter of prosperous merchant Samuel B. Miller, "the father of Fulton Fish Market," did nothing to hinder it. With his younger brother Seabury as an associate, he developed the firm of Caleb Haley & Company at 24 Fulton Market into one of the leading receivers and shippers of fish on the Atlantic Coast.

Caleb was wealthy, and most of his wealthy friends invested in expensive yachts to sail around the harbor. But Caleb was a farm boy at heart, and he decided to invest in a farm in his native town. He poured as much money into his farm as his friends did into their maritime hobbies, and he was fond of remarking that the farm was his yacht.

While living in New York Caleb had lost three young children to sickness, and he believed the country was the most healthful place to live. He also loved farming. In 1869, he purchased a portion of the old Winthrop farm for $12,000. For the rest of his life he enjoyed improving the land, maintaining its status as a year-round working farm. He invested in pigs, dairy cattle, poultry, horses and a span of working oxen, all of the finest stock.

The Haley Farm reached its prime at the end of the nineteenth and the beginning of the twentieth century, in contrast to many local farms that had been abandoned with the increasing emphasis on manufacturing. Originally the farm included a spacious farmhouse, which unfortunately burned in 1960. A live-in farmer and caretaker occupied part of this house, with the remainder reserved for the Haley family, who were in residence most of the summer. The dairy herd produced milk that was peddled daily in Noank village. Some of the distinctive Haley Farm milk bottles show up occasionally at flea markets.

Eons ago, glaciers had left huge boulders and plentiful rocks on Haley Farm. Caleb developed a hobby of building stone walls. Using a patented rock puller invented by Mystic native Captain George Washington Packer, he actively planned miles of carefully constructed stone walls, directing his crew as they laid down over three miles of sturdy barriers that still remain. Writing about the farm in 1982, Greg Stone noted, “Not a stone has fallen from place.”

Caleb delighted in entertaining city acquaintances and in demonstrating the virtues of life in the country. One visitor, Walter Hill, in October 1898 recorded his sojourn in a printed booklet tied with pale blue ribbon. Entitled *Haley Farm Souvenir*, this describes his visit while numerous photographs give us an idea of the buildings, the animals and the environs.

Haley Farm, once its proprietor’s pride, has changed since its heyday. The Haleys are no longer in residence. The prize animals are gone. The farmhouse, the barn, the corncribs and other outbuildings no longer stand, although their footprints may be seen. But the rolling fields bounded by Caleb’s impressive stone walls are there for all to enjoy, a memorial to the country boy who made good in the big city.

THE LEGACY OF FREDERIC BILL

For weeks I've been on the trail of Frederic Bill and his mansion. He was born on September 7, 1833, in Groton, although his birthplace now lies in Ledyard, which became an independent town in 1836. He spent his last years in Groton, too, on a farm purchased for his retirement. A philanthropist, he left the town two substantial landmarks—the Bill Memorial Library and Groton Heights School. With his wives, he is buried on the grounds behind the library.

Frederic was one of the five sons of Gurdon Bill Sr. As a young man he joined the family's publishing business. He traveled widely in Canada and the West, selling copies of *A History of the World* or *The Illustrated History of the Bible*. After the Civil War he left the book business, organizing the firm of Tracy & Bill in New York. They specialized in linen manufacture, but I've heard they really dealt in ladies undergarments. Whatever they sold, it was profitable. When Frederic Bill was forty, he was wealthy enough to retire to Groton.

He bought a sixty-three-acre farm from Erastus Avery for $6,500, signing the deed on May 21, 1875. This prime land lay along the Thames River near the summer home of his brother Gurdon. It spilled across "the new Eastern Point Road" adjacent to the railroad. According to the old deed, there was a schoolhouse on the property. With his wife, Lucy Denison Bill, Frederic settled happily at what became 443 Eastern Point Road. Their roomy, three-gabled mansion faced the road. It had several verandas and was covered with light gray clapboards and had green shutters. The north section was set aside for servants' quarters.

Philanthropist Frederic Bill established the Bill Memorial Library in 1888, presenting seventeen hundred books. The original building was dedicated in 1890.

In 1888, Bill made his first philanthropic move, purchasing seventeen hundred books to found Groton's first library in honor of his sisters, Eliza and Harriet. The new Bill Memorial Library building was dedicated on June 18, 1890. (Perhaps he was influenced by brother Henry, who had established a library in Ledyard in 1867.) Bill's first wife Lucy died in 1895, and the following year he married Julia O. Avery, Bill Memorial's first librarian. Ever generous, he contributed substantially to the new building of the First Church of Christ Congregational and completely financed the new brick Groton Heights School, replacing the old wooden building in 1912. He was also an early supporter of the establishment of Connecticut College.

In 1909, he sold nine acres of his valuable river property to Henry C. Rowe. This same land was acquired by Groton Iron Works in 1917, as a site for the manufacture of World War I steel freighters. It became the Victory Yard during World War II for submarine production and is now part of the Pfizer site.

In 1918, Frederic leased a large piece of his property, which he called "Bill Farm," to Chester Glidden for $250 a year. The tract lay across Eastern Point Road. Many people remember the Glidden dairy farm, as well as Joseph and Helen Glidden. This lease was renewed for many years, rising to $300 per annum in 1931.

The philanthropist died in Winter Park, Florida, on March 2, 1920, naming his wife Julia executor of his estate. She continued to live in the mansion, cared for by John and Martha Rankin, until her death in 1933. In her will, she made certain bequests to employees and friends, the Rankins and others, stipulating that the residue of her property should go to Connecticut College. Thus, in 1935, ownership of the Bill mansion and adjoining land went to the college, becoming rental property administered by Glenn Chapman, superintendent of buildings for the college.

The LaRoue family lived there for a long time, renting what had been the servants' quarters, while Professor George Avery of Connecticut College lived in the larger section. But in August 1940, the college sold the land and buildings to New London Terminal Corporation, which later leased it to Ballard Oil Company of Hartford for a tank farm for petroleum products.

When the property was sold, the LaRoues and Averys moved out. Later, Austin and Marie Battles and family moved into the mansion. Marie's father, Grover V. Lassen, was president of Ballard Oil, and Marie was secretary of the corporation. Then the LaRoues returned to their former apartment.

Bill LaRoue remembers how wonderful it was to live in those spacious quarters next to the Victory Yard, right on the river. Austin Battles was building a twenty-six-foot ketch in the barn. But that wasn't all that was under construction. Ballard Oil began building storage tanks, and they began to close in, coming nearer and nearer to the house. At last came the day when Mr. Grover Lassen himself tapped on the LaRoues' door and told them they would have to move. They planned to tear down the mansion to make room for more tanks. It was the end of an era and the end of Bill's mansion. The Battles family moved to Mystic, the LaRoues moved to Ledyard and the former Frederic Bill property now belongs to Amerada Hess Corporation.

THE DABOLL FAMILY AND THEIR HANDY ALMANAC

For nearly two centuries, Daboll's almanacs were essential to life in southern New England. No household would be without the current edition. A copy hung by every fireside. Farmers checked the little book every day for weather predictions, sunrise and sunset and auspicious times for planting crops. Fishermen and sailors depended on tidal tables. Housewives read the anecdotes and pleasantries. Advertisers offered all kinds of services for readers.

Sometimes the weather predictions didn't come true; Daboll missed predicting the 1938 hurricane by a mile. But, they were general enough to hit the mark more often than not. In the good old days, families consulted the almanac 365 days a year. They laughed when the sun was shining and Daboll promised rain, but they never missed a year's issue.

This unique publication, *The New England Almanac and Farmers' Friend*, was published in New London by the Daboll family continuously for 195 years. No other American almanac has approached that record.

The founder of the dynasty was Master Nathan Daboll, born at Center Groton in 1750. In his early life, he was a cooper, and according to tradition, he used the heads of the barrels he made to figure out problems in mathematics. He was a poor student at the classics, but he mastered arithmetic with the greatest of ease.

His expertise with numbers was well-known. He was soon in demand to train young Groton mariners in navigation and nautical astronomy. He is said to have taught those American seamen whose swift privateers made the British

The Daboll homestead in Center Groton where Master Nathan Daboll produced the *New England Almanac and Farmers' Friend*. *Courtesy of Jim Streeter.*

suffer during the Revolution. For years his school convened in his Center Groton homestead, which still stands. During the War of 1812, he conducted classes for midshipmen aboard the vessels of Decatur's fleet in New London Harbor. His own textbook, *Daboll's Practical Navigator*, was published posthumously in 1820. I own a prized copy that once belonged to Thomas W. Latham of Ledyard.

Master Nathan, critical of arithmetic texts in use in elementary schools of the time, decided to write one himself. The first edition of *Daboll's Complete Schoolmaster's Assistant* appeared in 1799 and was adopted widely in schools from Maine to South Carolina. This was one of the first texts to teach the American system of money in place of British pounds and pence.

In 1773, Timothy Green, a famed New London printer, produced *The Connecticut Almanac with Calculations by Nathan Daboll, Philomath*. This was the beginning of the famous series. The almanac's title varied, and at first, Daboll's name did not always appear on the title page, but the public knew it was his work. It finally became the *New England Almanac*, a publication prized for the accuracy of its computations. Some thought Master Nathan possessed supernatural powers to be able to predict eclipses and tides so accurately.

When Master Nathan died in 1818, the almanac passed to his son Nathan, known as "the Squire." Squire Nathan also continued the navigation school. He served as Groton town clerk, and later as judge of probate, in addition to preparing the yearly almanac.

After Squire Nathan died in 1863, Master Nathan's grandson, David A. Daboll, was ready to take over. And in 1897, the duty was assumed by the master's great-grandson, David Austin Daboll, known as David Aut to distinguish him from his father. For the 125th number of the almanac prepared by a Daboll, the cover depicted a facsimile of the 1773 issue.

In the present century, Loren Daboll had a hand in the almanac, but he preferred surveying and engineering to pure mathematics and turned the job over to his nephew, Ernest C. Daboll, who continued for more than thirty years.

When Ernest died on October 24, 1967, at the age of eighty-six, he was preparing the 1968 edition. There was no other Daboll willing to carry on. The almanac was sold to Robb Sagendorph, editor of *Yankee Magazine*, publisher of the rival *Old Farmer's Almanac*. Yankee agreed to bring out a token 1968 edition of the Daboll work and to include Daboll material in future editions of their own work.

So the Daboll dynasty and the Daboll almanac passed into history. Old copies often turn up at yard sales, and the items still make fascinating reading. The 1894 edition included an interesting explanation of a current problem:

> *According to Professor Littner, the eggs of a gypsy moth blew out the window from the collection of a naturalist 20 years ago, and the insects have increased till now they spread over a district in Massachusetts covering 200 square miles, where the desolation they have wrought is equal to that caused by fire or flood.*

There are also tips on how to keep wagon tires tight, how to find the latitude and an explanation of an eye affliction caused by continuous riding in streetcars. There are lists of lighthouses and Connecticut courts and tide tables calculated for the meridian of New London. For years the advertisement of T.A. Scott, submarine engineer and diver, took up the whole back cover.

Daboll's almanac had something for everyone.

MORTON PLANT AND THE GLAMOROUS GRISWOLD HOTEL

If you grew up in Groton, New London or Waterford, you remember The Griswold at Eastern Point. In its heyday, it was advertised as "the finest summer resort hotel in America." It was the epitome of elegance, a favorite convention spot and the center of high society during the Yale-Harvard boat races or New York Yacht Club regattas. It meant fine food, popular orchestras, latest fashions and money, money, money.

Millionaire Morton F. Plant caused The Griswold to be built. He moved into his new summer home, Branford House, in the summer of 1904 and began to look around the neighborhood. Eastern Point was a perfect place for a summer hotel. In 1846, Captain Silas Fiske built the Ocean House there. This vacation haven was later replaced by the Edgecomb House, and in 1884 the Sturdevants renovated this hotel and renamed it Fort Griswold House.

Fort Griswold House, with its choice harbor location, was popular for years, but when Morton Plant came to Eastern Point, it was shabby and no longer fashionable. Plant decided to buy the property and improve the neighborhood.

The old hotel opened as usual in June 1905 under the management of Benjamin H. Yard. About the same time, Plant announced plans to demolish the Fort Griswold House as soon as the season ended. He would replace it with a new hotel to be named Shennecossett Inn after the new golf course nearby. Plant's favorite architect, Robert William Gibson, designer of Branford House, would produce the design.

Tuesday, September 6, 1905, was a busy day at Fort Griswold House. While the last summer guests were departing, an auction was beginning. Throngs of bargain hunters bid on furnishings of the old hotel. Three thousand lots

The famous Griswold Hotel, noted summer resort, built by Morton F. Plant at Eastern Point in 1906.

of goods were offered. All day the steamer *Osprey* ferried crowds from New London. Meanwhile, both contractors and the architect waited impatiently to begin demolition. There was no time to be lost if the new building was to be ready the following June as Morton Plant had ordered.

On September 13, a miniature army under contractor Whipple of Norwich attacked the old hotel. The wide piazzas were demolished first. The interior was gutted and the tower soon came down. Whipple kept 140 men busy carrying out what the *New London Day* called "the second fall of Fort Griswold." Ten days later, nothing was left but stone foundations surrounded by debris and clouds of dust.

The stone masonry was eventually reused in the new work. By October 6, foundation walls were rising while building materials arrived by schooner. In December the inn grew as 125 carpenters worked, racing the weather. Steam heat and electric lights were installed.

When architect Gibson visited on December 28, he announced that the proposed name Shennecossett Inn would be dropped. He considered the Indian name too unwieldy for everyday use. The new hotel would be known as The Griswold, retaining enough of the old title to attract former guests.

Contractors finished their work on May 14, 1906, and the building was inspected by Plant. Manager B.H Yard had already arrived with his staff to supervise the laying of carpets. Billiard rooms were furnished in fine-grained quartered oak. Everything was of the best quality.

Under sunny skies on June 23, 1906, The Griswold opened formally to booming cannons and the applause of invited guests. Master Henry B. Plant, Morton's only son, broke out the large flag atop the one-hundred-foot flagpole on the front lawn. Two other flags were raised simultaneously from the roof. More than four hundred people witnessed the ceremonies. The new hotel, thanks to a miracle of construction, was ready in just 225 days.

The Griswold was so popular that in August would-be guests had to be turned away. The following October, an addition was commenced on the south side, a new wing to accommodate eighty more guests. In September 1909, work began on a three-story Griswold annex, which would include sixty more elegant rooms, on the opposite side of Avery Avenue. There was a third addition in 1916.

Plant developed a successful Florida hotel, the Belleview at Belleair, which shared The Griswold's staff and orchestra in winter. For years both were managed by H.D. Saxton. Many slick, well-illustrated brochures advertised the twin hostelries. Regretfully, they always located The Griswold in New London rather than in Groton, where it belonged.

During the Great Depression, The Griswold's popularity waned. Big wooden hotels were no longer in vogue, and lifestyles were changing. After several attempts to revive its elegance, the property was sold to the Pfizer pharmaceutical firm. The huge, sprawling wooden structure was razed in 1969. I was among the mourners.

The vacant site overlooking the Thames, which still offers a magnificent harbor view, is now part of Groton's municipal golf course. But it's hard to imagine the hum of activity, the throngs of well-dressed patrons, the bright lights and the music that once made the spot an elegant and popular summer hotel.

THE LEGENDS OF MORTON PLANT

In June 1904, Morton F. Plant inherited $14.6 million from the estate of his father, Henry B. Plant, who had made his money creating a huge empire of Florida steamship lines and railroads along with luxurious hotels. In 1904, a dollar bought considerably more than it does today, with income taxes that were far less demanding.

At his death, Morton Plant's estate was inventoried at over $34 million. He had devoted his life to enjoying this hefty fortune. He was more than generous with his money, especially to the Town of Groton, where he had built his lavish summer home, Branford House, a mansion now part of the University of Connecticut campus at Avery Point.

When the charismatic millionaire came to this area, newspapers loved him. He made plenty of headlines. Reporters outlined his latest philanthropies and told of his expensive yachts and the world-famous celebrities he entertained. He was a legend in his time, and over the years stories about him have become legends in themselves. It is often hard to separate fact from fiction.

There is the matter of New London Ledge Light. Some time ago, an article appeared stating that Plant had built that lighthouse to use as a guesthouse when Branford House overflowed with celebrities. This was not true—New London Ledge Light was erected at Southwest Ledge with money appropriated by Congress, first exhibiting a light in 1910. Plant had nothing to do with it.

Legendary Morton Plant, once Groton's most famous resident, built a summer home at Avery Point at the turn of the century. *Courtesy of Jim Streeter.*

It is true that Plant planned to excel at everything he did. In his greenhouses he raised beautiful flowers for his mansion, as well as for The Griswold Hotel, which he had built to smarten up the neighborhood in which he lived. In November 1917, his chrysanthemums captured seventeen first- and eight second-place prizes in a New York flower show. The winning blooms were later distributed to city hospitals.

One of Plant's favorite philanthropies was Connecticut College. There is the story that Plant gave $1 million in cash to start the institution. Some say he brought it down from Hartford in a little black satchel. There is truth in this, I think, because Gertrude Noyes relates a similar anecdote in her carefully researched history of the college.

Plant's first wife, whom he married in 1888, was Nellie Capron of Baltimore. An architectural student, she helped design Bradford House with Robert W. Gibson, an English architect. Nellie died of typhoid fever at the mansion on August 7, 1913.

Plant married again, and there are legends about his second marriage to Mrs. Selden Manwaring of New London. Authors Taylor and Colcord, in their book, *The Belleview Midor Resort Hotel*, write,

> *When Morton Plant met the married Maisie Cadwell Manwaring he was so bewitched he offered her husband $8 million to divorce her… She became Maisie Manwaring Plant and Morton gained custody of her son Philip whom he later adopted.*

On the other hand, in Morton Plant's obituary, the *New London Day* noted, "On June 18, 1914 he married Mrs. Sarah May Cadwell Manwaring of this city. It was reported at the time that Mr. Plant's bridal gift to his wife was $8 million." I'll let you decide who got the money.

The entrance to the Plant estate, Branford House, at Avery Point in Groton.

Then there's the question of his New York town house. In 1905, with his summer home at Avery Point complete, Plant purchased from William K. Vanderbilt the property now known as 651 Fifth Avenue, diagonally across from Vanderbilt's home. Plant agreed that it would not be used for commercial purposes for at least twenty-five years. He employed his favorite architect, Robert W. Gibson, to design a six-story marble and granite palazzo in the neo–Italian Renaissance style. He enjoyed it for a while, but as time went on, he was troubled by increasing commercial development and decided to move uptown to Fifth Avenue and Eighty-sixth Street.

By dickering with Vanderbilt, he was able to arrange to sell his building to Cartier, the famous jeweler, the firm that occupies the building today. A notable architectural landmark known for its lavish decorations at Christmastime, it is the last truly elegant mansion in the area and has been called "the jewel of Fifth Avenue."

Plant sold it in 1917 for $1.2 million. Instead of taking cash, he took it out in trade. He exchanged the building for jewelry that had caught his new wife's fancy, a two-strand natural oriental pearl necklace. A photo of Maisie wearing the pearls, accented by her plunging neckline, shows them to be rather large and perhaps not appealing to modern tastes, but Maisie loved them.

Today, Cartier's at 651 Fifth Avenue, completely refurbished in 2001, is one of the most desirable commercial sites in the world, valued at upwards of $26 million. Situated at the entrance to Fifth Avenue, it is one of New York's most famous buildings. But pearls are not as fashionable now as they were in 1917. It has been estimated that Maisie's necklace would be worth only $26,000 today, making it a poor bargain.

ABBY DAY SLOCOMB

She Made a Difference

Abby Day Slocomb, or more formally, Mrs. Cuthbert Harrison Slocomb, was brought up in the grace and courtliness of New Orleans. She made quite a stir when she bought a house in Groton in 1888 and turned her attention to the Revolutionary War battlefield just across the street. Before she left, she had established a chapter of the Daughters of the American Revolution, organized their museum, convinced the state of Connecticut to purchase the land around old Fort Griswold for a state park and created a design for the Connecticut state flag.

Abby's ancestors came from New England. Her great-grandfather, Captain Elisha Hinman, was a successful New London privateer during the Revolution. His wife, Abigail Dolbeare, born in Norwich, had distinguished herself on the awful day of September 6, 1781, during the British attack on New London. When she met her old acquaintance Benedict Arnold burning the town, she threatened him with a gun. Abby cut her teeth on stories of Abigail's bravery.

Captain Hinman's daughter Hannah married Captain James Day, a brave mariner of the War of 1812, who deliberately wrecked his vessel off Point Judith to prevent its capture by the British. James took his family south to New Orleans "on behalf of his lungs," in search of a healthier climate. His oldest son, James Ingersoll Day, married a Quaker, Sarah Armitage. The couple had five daughters and two sons. Abby, the oldest, was born in 1838.

Abby's father loved New England. When his business flourished, he built a lavish summer residence in Stonington in 1851. Called Walnut Grove, it stood on the site of the present Admiral Fife Naval Recreation Area north of Route 1. Here the family escaped the summer heat of

Abby Day Slocum's great-grandmother, Abigail Hinman, defies the traitor Benedict Arnold during the burning of New London, September 6, 1781.

New Orleans, while the father busied himself as president of the New York, Providence and Boston Railroad.

In New Orleans, Abby married Cuthbert Harrison Slocomb, owner of a prosperous hardware business. Their only child, Cora, was born in 1862. As the Civil War raged, Abby's husband served as captain in the Confederate army. He was badly wounded at Richmond as he carried dispatches to General Robert E. Lee. Abby, nursing behind the lines, found her husband among her patients and brought him home to recover.

Cuthbert died in 1873, leaving Abby very well off. She devoted herself to her daughter. Cora was extremely popular, chosen as Rex's queen in the Mardi Gras in 1880. She studied abroad, and in Rome she fell in love with a wealthy Italian count, Detalmo di Brazzi. She was twenty-five; he was forty-three. They were married in 1887 and Cora went to live on a huge estate in Italy, where she flew the American flag daily.

With her daughter happily married, Abby came to Groton and bought and renovated a large house on Monument Street that she called "Daisy Crest over Groton." The home is now remodeled into condominiums. She concerned herself with the new National Society of the Daughters of the American Revolution (NSDAR). She had already been appointed regent for Groton and Stonington by national officers. On September 13, 1893, she invited sixteen local ladies to her home to form a new chapter. She had hoped to name the chapter for Abigail Hinman, but by vote of the members the choice was Anna Warner Bailey, Groton's famous heroine. It was a rare occasion when Abby didn't get her way.

Under Abby's firm guidance, the new NSDAR chapter restored the old caretaker's house beside the monument, creating a small museum for historic memorabilia. She entertained lavishly for chapter affairs, secured a state appropriation for the Monument House, organized the first Connecticut chapter of Children of the American Revolution and was tireless in her patriotic efforts.

In 1895, she petitioned Congress to purchase land surrounding Fort Griswold. To speed up the process, she and her wealthy friends bought up several tracts to hold until it was finally turned over to the state in 1903. She was generous with her own funds and devised ways for the chapter to raise money, ranging from an elaborate Fairy Masque presented at the Lyceum theater in New London to the sale of souvenir china and photographs at the Monument House. She was never shy about asking her friends for donations.

When she discovered there was no official design for the Connecticut state flag, she bent her efforts to that project and did not rest until one was adopted. She employed a secretary to type her voluminous correspondence, copies of which are on file in the safe of the Anna Warner Bailey Chapter, NSDAR, in the Monument House.

Her vigorous Groton regime ended abruptly with her daughter's serious mental illness in 1906. Mrs. Slocomb left at once for Europe and no longer spent time at Daisy Crest over Groton. It was reported that Cora had "lost her mind" suddenly while having a gown fitted. The cause of her dementia was never clearly diagnosed, and she never recovered.

Mrs. Slocomb spent her last years with her ailing daughter. But her legacy, the state park at Fort Griswold and the Monument House Museum, remain a memorial to her proud American heritage.

QUASH WILLIAMS

His Story

February is Black History Month, a time to remember important people and events in African American history. To find a local hero we need look no farther than Mystic's ancient Whitehall Cemetery, the final resting place of the famed and beloved Quash Williams. Born a slave, he rose to be a lay preacher in Groton's thriving Second Baptist Church. He made such a lasting impression that decades after his death he was honored with a marble slab placed on his grave by public subscription.

He was born on December 15, 1762, in the household of Colonel John Williams of Stonington. Like his father before him, he was called Quash, a name of African origin meaning "Sunday." As was the custom in the eighteenth century, he took his master's surname. As a slave, he had no formal education. He said that all the learning he had came from carrying the Williams children on his back to the schoolhouse

In 1786, his life changed. Elder Silas Burrows of Groton's church at the crest of Fort Hill held a series of fiery revival meetings, converting a host of sinners. Quash was among them. After this experience he became the elder's right-hand man, a sincere and popular leader in the congregation. His opinion was sought in all church matters.

The State of Connecticut had passed legislation in 1784 that led to the freeing of many slaves. In March 1795, John Williams, the great-grandson of the colonel, signed Quash's manumission papers:

> *I, John Williams of Stonington, having a negro man by the name of Quash about 30 years old, propose to free him, if the selectmen agree, upon the following conditions, viz., the said Quash to serve and faithfully behave himself, be subject to my orders and attentive to my business until the 25th of next December, and then he is to be his own free man; unless said Quash be sick and then he is to make up the lost time when wanted.*

Quash fulfilled his obligations and was freed, with more time to devote to church affairs. The Second Baptist Church included many black members. In 1819, the year after the death of Elder Silas, he was appointed their designated church leader. In those days the church had considerable influence over its flock, supervising every aspect of their lives. Those who broke the rules became the subject of labor to bring them back to the straight and narrow. They had to account to the church for the error of their ways.

Baptists were strait-laced and serious then. From church records we know that Quash was appointed to call on Sister Juno when it was reported that she sang for young people to dance, behavior considered unacceptable. In spite of kindly Quash's intercession, the unfortunate woman was excluded from the fellowship "for aiding in frolicking and for singing and dancing in her home."

Groton's Second Baptist Church on Fort Hill, where Quash Williams was a lay preacher.

Quash was famed for preaching sage sermons and offering fervent prayer, as well as for providing wholesome advice to parishioners. His motto was "walk as well as talk," to live by the gospel. He demonstrated Christian virtues and was universally loved and cherished for his work and counsel. The congregation mourned when he died on November 2, 1830. He was laid to rest in quiet Whitehall Burying Ground, where the John Williams family had buried their dead for more than a century. His wife Hannah lies at his side. Nearby is his daughter Delancy, who married Silas Hazard. A second daughter was the wife of Jabez Prince Niles of Indian Town, Ledyard.

The marble slab placed on his grave in 1866 bears the words, "Old Quash was truly an example, and by it, yet being dead, he speaketh." The old church on Fort Hill is no more, but memories of Quash Williams and his way of life remain with us today.

ALBERT G. STARK AND THE OCTAGON HOUSE

Albert Gallatin Stark died of dysentery in 1853 when he was only twenty-nine years old, but he packed a lot of living into those years. The home he built, a unique octagon house on West Mystic Avenue in Mystic, is one of the architectural treasures of the town of Groton.

He was born on May 6, 1824, the son of Sanford Stark and Nancy Park, a direct descendant of Will Stark, one of Groton's earliest settlers.

He was educated at Portersville Academy, where his talent for public speaking and original writing made him the talk of the village. He became a prosperous merchant in the village of Mystic River as proprietor of a large general store on Noank Road, which was also the site of the post office. He devoted time to civic affairs, serving as a Groton selectman, representative to the General Assembly and judge of probate. In 1852, he ran for Congress on the Free Soil ticket, and although he failed to get elected, he received substantial local support.

A.G. Stark was the heart and soul of the Mystic Lyceum, an organization sponsoring public programs and entertainment. He used his considerable talent in writing for its presentations. Naturally, he read all the latest publications and became acquainted with the work of Orson S. Fowler, whose book, entitled *The Octagon House: A Home for All*, was a bestseller of the time. Stark saw Fowler's home on a visit to the Hudson River and was so impressed that he had an octagon house erected for his family in a new real estate development now known as West Mystic Avenue. Two years later, his brother, Captain Henry Stark, built a fine Italianate home just to the north.

Orson Squire Fowler profoundly influenced American architecture of the time, but he was not a builder by trade. He was involved with phrenology, a nineteenth-century pseudoscience that claimed to be able to determine character, personality traits and even criminality by the shape of a person's head. It was popularly known as "reading bumps." Its advocates believed that thirty-seven faculties could be "read" on the crania. Orson and his younger brother, Lorenzo Niles Fowler, were leading practitioners and were internationally famous.

Educated at Amherst College, Orson was an eccentric and original thinker. In addition to phrenology, he turned his attention toward a new concept in building. He published his material in 1848, introducing several revolutionary ideas. He advocated the octagon shape for homes, believing it to be more economical for space, admitting increased sunlight and facilitating communication between rooms. Among other advanced ideas, he championed indoor toilets and hot-water furnaces. He also believed that every man could be his own architect and gave detailed instructions for constructing mortar for the gravel walls he used for the octagon. He personally built his own three-story, sixty-room octagon residence overlooking the Hudson River at Fishkill, New York, keeping careful account of his expenses.

Lured by the attractive façade and promises of increased good health, all over the country people began building octagon houses, as well as eight-sided barns and outhouses. Fowler's plans appealed to the imagination, and several thousand such buildings were constructed. A number still survive.

Stark's house was built in 1850 and must have been an exciting home for his family. Four years before, on March 1, 1846, he had married Hannah Williams Wolfe, daughter of Captain George Wolfe. Their daughter Sarah was born in 1847. Two sons, Albert Henry Stark and William Ledyard Stark, were born after they moved in. The original house was most impressive, with an octagonal cupola and fancy roof balustrade, plus elaborate porch trim. Many of these details survived until the devastating 1938 hurricane.

Sadly, Albert Stark had less than three years in this home before his death on September 29, 1853. This remarkable and talented man is buried in Lower Mystic Cemetery. In Groton Probate Records, I found an inventory of his estate, including the entire contents of his store—dry goods, clothes, pails, tumblers and boots—the whole works. He also owned shares in four Mystic vessels, including the ship *Harriet Hoxie*, and twenty shares of Mystic River bank stock valued at $1,200.00. The entire estate amounted to $16,173.28, a huge sum for the day. Too bad he didn't live longer to enjoy it.

His widow continued to occupy the octagon house. In 1860, she married Captain Isaac Washington, who had commanded a number of Mystic sailing vessels. Her son, William Ledyard Stark, born and brought up in the octagon house, moved west when he was twenty. A lawyer, he eventually located in Aurora, Nebraska, and was elected to Congress for three terms.

Through the years, many people have lived in the octagon house that A.G. Stark built, including State Senator Cathy Cook. The house is looking very well right now, carefully restored, approximating the glory envisioned by its builder.

WHO WAS THOMAS ROGERS?

The name Thomas Rogers didn't ring a bell with me when I found him listed as a famous Groton native. I have studied Groton history for a long time, but I had never come across Thomas before. Apparently he was a locomotive designer and builder who lived from 1792 to 1856.

When I investigated, I found plenty of information about him. His Rogers Locomotive Works was second only to the famous Baldwin firm in production. A colleague said that he had done more for the modern American locomotive than any of his contemporaries. Why, then, is he unknown in his native town?

The answer to that is easy. He moved away from Groton at the start of the War of 1812. He was born in Groton on March 16, 1792, a lineal descendant of the Thomas Rogers who came to America on the *Mayflower* in 1620. Our Thomas grew up in Groton, did some blacksmithing and was apprenticed early to learn the trade of house carpenter. When the war began, he moved to Paterson, New Jersey, a town where manufacturing prospered, aiming to provide the country with goods formerly imported from England. As a journeyman carpenter he found plenty of work.

His first job was making patterns for power looms that manufactured cotton duck, replacing imported British textiles. Showing the initiative that characterized his life, he soon bought the patent from his boss and, with a partner, began to manufacture the looms himself. Ten years later he owned a mill employing two hundred hands spinning cotton and building machinery. In time his looms were so much in demand that he gave up textile manufacture.

In 1832, he moved to a different site, forming a new firm, Rogers, Ketchum and Grosvenor. A new railroad from Jersey City to Paterson was under construction nearby. The locomotive, built in England, had been shipped to America in pieces. Thomas Rogers took this opportunity to study it, making drawings and patterns of each piece. Eager to enter a new field, he soon built his own engine, the Sandusky, filing for his own patent for improved driving wheels in 1837. He sold the engine to the Erie Railroad for $6,750.

Now that American-built locomotives were available, orders poured in for Rogers's models. It took eighteen months for him to complete the first engine, but he produced seven the following year. His engines grew bigger and better and his plant expanded. In 1845, he built a fine passenger engine, the Springfield, for the Hartford and New Haven Railroad. One of his innovations, counterbalanced driving wheels, was hailed as a remarkable advancement in transportation and was widely adopted.

Thomas Rogers died in New York on April 19, 1856, leaving his firm in the hands of his son Jacob. The Rogers Locomotive Works went on to expand until it employed two thousand people in 1890, Baldwin's closest rival. With such a record, this modest Groton native deserves a little more publicity.

ABOUT TOWN

JEMIMA'S ROCK

The Woman Behind the Groton Landmark

Hikers along the trails in Groton's serene and green Haley Farm are sure to notice a huge split boulder on the brow of a ledge left eons ago by the glaciers. For centuries it has been called Jemima's Rock. Even earlier, this conspicuous landmark was noticed by Native Americans as they cleared their fields in Poquonnock.

John Winthrop Jr., founder of Pequot Plantation (later New London), knew it as "canopie rock," and as such it is noted in the seventeenth-century document that granted him a huge piece of Poquonnock real estate extending through Bluff Point and Groton Long Point, including Haley Farm. The boulder's form suggests a colonial church pulpit overhung with a canopy or sounding board, a primitive public address system to carry the preacher's message to every corner of the meetinghouse.

The name Jemima's Rock commemorates eccentric Jemima Wilkinson, the first American-born woman to found a religious society. According to local legend, this remarkable spirit once preached from the Haley Farm boulder, probably during a visit to Groton in 1787 documented by entries in local diaries. We know she preached in the Second Baptist Church on top of Fort Hill, defying and irritating its pastor, Elder Silas Burrows. It is perfectly possible that she also addressed the public from the rock not far away. It would have been right in character.

Born in 1752 among the Quakers in Cumberland, Rhode Island, Jemima led a commonplace life until October 1776, when she experienced a spiritual rebirth and a religious conversion that she likened to the resurrection of Lazarus. After a long illness, during which she lay in a trance, she arose and proclaimed herself the Publick Universal Friend. She launched her ministry, preaching a better life, converting her own family first and branching out into surrounding towns. Among her followers were Jedediah Holmes of Stonington, Latham Avery and Richard Smith of Groton and the five sons of Benjamin Brown, all pillars of their communities.

A young schoolmaster, James Woodbridge from Gallup Hill in Ledyard, went to hear her at the Groton home of Benjamin Brown. He wrote

Jemima's Rock, famous Groton landmark on Haley Farm, where Jemima Wilkinson is said to have preached.

about her in his diary. "Went to hear the Friend think high of herself, assume highly," he noted, apparently not much impressed.

Stonington, Groton and New London proved fruitful fields for her mission. She converted many and attracted followers with her forceful personality. In the 1780s it was startling to hear any woman preach. That placed her in the limelight and established her as a figure of legend. Many myths arose. It was said that she declared herself the reincarnation of Christ in woman's form, although she herself never made that claim. There were rumors that she rose from her coffin to preach three days after her death from a fatal fever, and it was said that she could raise the dead.

Sweeping aside the folklore, Jemima Wilkinson remains a colorful figure. She was a strong, athletic woman who rode a spirited horse, sitting erect in her sidesaddle. Her habits of cleanliness, unique in the eighteenth century, caused suspicion. She washed her long black hair daily and never powdered it in Martha Washington style. She wore it long about her shoulders, and in the days when no woman was considered properly dressed without a frilly white cap, she went bareheaded. She knew how to attract attention.

She was an eloquent speaker, charming audiences with her warm voice and quoting long passages of scripture and portions of the Quaker writings of George Fox and William Penn. Everywhere the Publick Universal Friend attracted large crowds of enthusiastic hearers. It is quite likely that she did preach from Jemima's Rock, exhorting her listeners to shun evil and quoting scriptures as the spirit moved her.

Jemima was a nonconformist, and her unorthodox manner soon brought opposition. She was charged with fraud and blasphemy, and there were accusations of sexual promiscuity because of her attentive home ministry to certain wealthy male converts. She became a very controversial figure.

Seeking escape from her critics and dreaming of a religious community of her faithful followers, Jemima and about 260 adherents finally left New England for the wilderness of upper New York State. The area where she settled is in the Finger Lakes region about fifty miles southwest of Rochester. There they founded what became the town of Penn Yan. Her followers also established a mill near Seneca Lake, using millstones brought from Connecticut. Her last home still stands in the township of Jerusalem, where she died of edema in 1819.

She was buried privately and the exact place of her grave is still a secret. Her letters and journals were also hidden away, and only recently were made available for research. A biography by Herbert A. Wisbey Jr., *Pioneer Prophetess: Jemima Wilkinson, the Publick Universal Friend*, appeared in 1964.

The Universal Friend is still remembered in the communities she founded, and her memory lingers at Groton's Haley Farm with Jemima's Rock.

RAILROAD FERRIES CROSS THE THAMES

In the 1850s, when railroads were the most modern and comfortable way to travel, engineers were faced with one great obstacle in their efforts to establish a shoreline route from Boston to New York. The Thames River between Groton and New London was wide and deep, and until technology advanced, there was no way a railroad bridge could be built across that river.

Awaiting that happy day, planners arrived at a workable solution. In 1856, the Connecticut legislature granted a charter to the New Haven, New London and Stonington Railroad, authorizing the company to operate a route from New Haven to New London, to construct tracks westward from Stonington to Groton Bank and to cross the broad Thames with a steam railroad ferry. Cars with passengers aboard would

Railroad ferries *Thames River* and *Groton*, about 1876. These vessels carried railroad cars across the harbor before the bridge was built. *Courtesy of Jim Streeter.*

roll onto the ferry to travel across the harbor. On the other side, those cars would be connected to another locomotive and continue the trip.

On the Connecticut River, the ferry *Shaumpishuh* had shuttled cars between Saybrook and Lyme since July 1852, a convenience well received by passengers.

For the Thames River route, the George Greenman & Company shipyard, at the present site of Mystic Seaport Museum, was building a 357-ton wooden vessel named *Shore Line.* The 125-foot steamer wasn't ready when the railroad opened for traffic on December 30, 1858. It was nearly a year before the ferry was completed, and in the interim, passengers had to alight from the train carrying their baggage to board the old side-wheeler *Eastern Rail Road* and transfer to the opposite shore.

The New London railroad landing was near the station at The Parade. On the eastern shore, the Groton ferry slip stood at what is now the site of General Dynamics–Electric Boat Company's old North Yard. Eventually, the railroad built an eight-stall brick roundhouse by the slip where locomotives could be turned.

The *Shore Line*'s first official crossing on Monday, December 12, 1859, was part of a New Haven to Boston trial run. Twenty-five special guests boarded the train at New Haven at 2:30 p.m. At 4:00 p.m. they arrived at New London, where their car was quickly rolled aboard the new ferry. While crossing the harbor, guests devoured a hasty meal. Within fifteen minutes, the special was on its way to Boston, arriving at 9:00 p.m.

To travel between New York and Boston over this shoreline route required eight and a half hours, but 150 passengers made the journey during the first week of service.

The ferry *Shore Line* had a single track amidships that could handle two cars per crossing. The locomotive was not carried aboard. A different engine waited for the cars at the other ferry slip. This river crossing service was so successful that by 1867 the ferry had to be lengthened fifty feet so three cars could be carried.

In 1871, this original vessel was retired, replaced by the 183-foot steamer *Thames River* built at Greenport, Long Island, by Henry Steers. Registering 882 gross tons and boasting double tracks, the new ferry carried five cars. On the upper deck was a spacious dining room where passengers could dine while crossing the harbor. Railroad ferries had made the Shoreline Railroad the shortest and quickest route between New York and Boston.

The *Thames River*'s maiden voyage on July 27, 1871, was marred by stormy weather, but four hundred guests enjoyed a cruise upriver to the new navy yard. P.S. Gilmore's famous band entertained them as they squeezed around tables in the dining saloon to enjoy food served by uniformed stewards.

Bulky railroad ferries were not easy to handle in strong winds or blizzards, but service was surprisingly reliable. The *Thames River* didn't miss a trip in five years, rolling up forty-one thousand miles crossing and recrossing the harbor. But soon, in the name of the progress, a new vessel came to the river.

The larger railroad ferry *Groton* began service on May 24, 1877. Also built by Steers, the rugged 253-foot vessel had 42-foot paddlewheels driven by a three-hundred-horsepower engine. There were lounges for ladies and gentlemen and a plush restaurant on the upper deck, but the huge *Groton* was laid up in winter while the smaller *Thames River* took over the run.

Captain George H. Eldredge of Mystic often commanded the *Groton* when it crossed the river. The son of *Shore Line*'s first captain, he had also piloted the *Thames River* and the spare boats *Eastern Rail Road* and *Union*.

When engineers were finally able to build a bridge across the Thames, the dream of an uninterrupted rail link between Boston and New York came true. The $1.6 million drawbridge ended the usefulness of railroad ferries.

On opening day, October 10, 1889, the river was crowded with vessels, while special trains from each direction approached the spans, waiting as the draw swung open. The ferry *Groton* passed upstream through the east passage, rounded the open draw and returned through the west passage while a band aboard played "Auld Lang Syne." Then the steel draw swung into position and the trains crossed. The shoreline route was complete.

The old ferries *Groton* and *Thames River* were sold to a Chesapeake Bay company and departed New London on November 26, 1889. The *Groton* was destroyed by fire off Virginia, but the *Thames River* ran as a railroad ferry until 1896.

Thus railroad ferries on the Thames passed into history.

THE FIRST THAMES RIVER BRIDGE

It wasn't easy to build a railroad bridge across the wide Thames River. The span was vital to complete a shoreline railroad route between Boston and New York, but for years, such a structure was impossible. By 1881, when there were rumors that at last the Thames would be bridged, New London residents reacted angrily. They thought a bridge across the river would ruin their maritime trade by obstructing navigation to Norwich. Furthermore, it would spoil the beautiful scenic river—all to save thirty minutes on the Boston run.

The first railroad bridge across the Thames River was built in 1889 and served for thirty years. *Courtesy of Jim Streeter.*

Congress authorized the bridge in spite of these bitter protests, although construction was delayed until 1888. The new bridge required one of the longest spans yet attempted in nineteenth-century America—a 1,423-foot steel superstructure. The 503-foot draw with a steam-powered turntable would permit two passages for vessels, allowing a 32-foot headway. The bridge was built at the harbor's narrowest point, just below Winthrop's Neck.

From the start, soft oozing mud on the river bottom made construction difficult. Heavy piles for the three main piers were driven through the muck until they hit hardpan, requiring depths of 103, 128 and 138 feet.

Bridge construction methods had not achieved today's sophisticated technology. Testing procedures were devised as work progressed. When stone pier foundations were built up to height, engineers tested the strength of the center pier, which supported the draw as well as passing trains. They piled tons of pig iron on top of the pier, more than the estimated weight it would have to bear. When the pier proved solid, complicated steelwork began.

The New York, Providence and Boston Railroad financed the structure, which cost $1.6 million. It also provided tracks to connect with the new span, for tracks from Providence ended at the present General Dynamics location some distance south of the bridge. To correct this, it laid five miles of double track from Poquonnock, blasting through granite ledges.

By early October 1889, everything was ready. Private tests for the bridge were arranged for October 6. They were supposed to be secret, but word got around. By 9:30 a.m., four hundred curious onlookers were present.

A test train with six locomotives arrived from Providence, pulling nine passenger cars bulging with railroad workmen. At the signal, a giant forty-ton locomotive inched onto the bridge. The other engines and cars cautiously ventured a short distance onto the east span, then backed off. The structure held, so the test train crawled slowly to the middle of the draw, stopped a few minutes, then proceeded confidently across the entire trestle.

Now that more than six hundred tons had passed safely over the new bridge, construction engineers declared that it could withstand an earthquake. It was ready for use.

Opening ceremonies were held on October 10, 1889, a cool, sunny autumn day. Spectators lined riverbanks and crowded the bluff at East New London. All sorts of vessels thronged the harbor. Steamers displayed flags and bunting. Small craft sculled or sailed about.

At 1:15 p.m., a special train from New York reached New London drawn by Engine No. 10, with Joseph Miner at the throttle. City officials, newsmen and invited dignitaries swarmed aboard at the station. The train crossed the river and puffed on to Poquonnock, where a train from Boston was waiting.

Both trains proceeded side by side over the double tracks to the east bridge approach. There they waited while the old railroad ferry *Groton* circled slowly through the draw, officially opening the bridge. The span closed and the two trains passed majestically, side by side, across the new structure and steamed slowly into the New London station.

Whistles blew, bells rang and spectators cheered. A new era had arrived. Passengers on the shoreline route would no longer have to bother with railroad ferries.

To celebrate this milestone, six hundred gentlemen guests boarded the steamer *Connecticut* for a banquet luncheon at 3:00 p.m., welcomed aboard by courteous officers of the Stonington line wearing their best uniforms, complete with white gloves. Dining tables filled the main deck as well as the ladies' cabin below.

All kinds of delicacies were served—oysters on the half shell, consommé, salmon, roast beef, turkey, tongue and chicken, as well as lobster and potato salads with relishes, olives and chowchow. The bounteous meal ended with assorted desserts and coffee, while railroad officials and politicians provided speeches suitable for the occasion.

Regular passenger trains began to use the bridge on November 14, 1889, making the Boston–New York run much smoother and quicker. This railroad drawbridge served the trains for thirty years, until a new span opened in 1919. Then the original 1889 bridge was converted to a highway bridge for the use of autos, trolleys and pedestrians. It was a welcome change for those who had depended on the ferry.

POQUONNOCK'S DRIVING PARK

Don't Call It a Racetrack!

Few people have heard that there was once a racetrack in Groton, about half a mile east of the town hall on the present Route 1, just across from Poquonnock Plains Park. In 1891, sporting men who loved to drive spirited horses at top speed incorporated the Groton Driving Park in the village of

The Groton Driving Park, shown here in 1896, drew large crowds to see horse racing and later automobile racing. *Courtesy of the Mystic Seaport Museum.*

Poquonnock Bridge to promote horse racing and other athletic sports. The park was also used for motorcycle and auto races and for baseball games.

Nothing in the peaceful scene today, the location of Fort Hill homes and Sutton Park, recalls the racetrack. However, a recent gift to the Town of Groton by Dr. Ellicott McConnell of Easton, Maryland, is proof positive that this track did exist and was the scene of many a thrilling contest. Dr. McConnell had in his possession a trophy, a silver loving cup that his father, Christie McConnell, won at a Poquonnock meet driving an Oldsmobile. Made by the Knickerbocker Silver Company, the cup is nicely inscribed, stating that it was presented by the Autogenous Welding Company.

In 1891, some worthy citizens considered horse racing not quite proper. Therefore the track was always called the Driving Park. The controlling company sold one hundred shares in the enterprise at twenty-five dollars each. It leased twenty acres of level land from Henry Gardiner, once part of the John Winthrop estate, and built a fine half-mile racetrack, a judges' stand and a grandstand that would seat six hundred, with fourteen box stalls for the horses at the south side. Inside the oval track the company laid out a baseball diamond. At the grand opening on September 2, 1892, a crowd of one thousand nosily enjoyed trotting races, bicycle races and the baseball game. It cost fifty cents to sit in the grandstand, and music was furnished by the Stonington Band.

The *New London Day* provided excellent coverage of the race program, announcing the winners and their prizes in the sporting section and noting with approval the varied events. The park offered a good race program. Sometimes attendance was so high that crowds of horsemen caused a huge traffic jam on the Groton–New London ferry. When the Groton and Stonington Street Railway began to run trolley cars in 1904, many people took advantage of this new transportation to attend the meets. It was a popular weekend amusement.

The Driving Park had its ups and downs through the years, with many a change in management and procedure, but 1914 was its finest season. Two thousand spectators turned up for Memorial Day, when the stables were decorated with bunting and stands were crowded with women and children. Five thousand flocked to the park on the Fourth of July to see Flying George Bittner win the motorcycle races. Also, according to the *New London Day*, the crowd watched an automobile race between an Oldsmobile and a Pierce Arrow.

This was probably the race in which Christie McConnell won the silver trophy. Oddly enough, there is no date on the cup, but we know that Christie, who was nineteen years old at the time, was driving an Oldsmobile. Its original owner drove that car in the Long Island Vanderbilt Cup Race. Later, after he rolled over the car in an accident that killed his wife, he sold the car to Christie.

Whatever the date, Christie was wearing the proper automobile costume for the occasion—a duster with cap and goggles much like Barney Oldfield, the famous racing driver who was nicknamed "the Mile-a-Minute Man." In 1914, sixty miles an hour was considered highly dangerous, but Christie achieved that speed on the oval dirt track at the foot of Fort Hill and went home with trophy.

If 1914 was the park's finest season, it was also regrettably its last. World War I raged in Europe and the Driving Park never regained the excitement of that summer. There were no more automobile races, and nature reclaimed the ground. In 1917, owner Henry Gardiner began a logging operation to provide timber for the Groton Iron Works, where vessels were constructed for the war effort. Horses and autos vanished from the oval track, although its form could be seen on aerial photos in the 1930s.

Yet the silver loving cup survived, and happily found its way back to Groton. Christie's son Ellicott and his daughter, now Elizabeth McConnell Haddad of North Stonington, grew up in the Groton area. Ellicott graduated from Robert E. Fitch High School in 1941. Recently he asked his classmate, Malcolm F. Brown, to find a suitable home for his father's trophy. This was not easy to do. Groton is home to several historical societies, namely Noank, Mystic River and Groton Bank, but there is no society or museum devoted exclusively to Groton memorabilia.

The problem was solved by Barbara Tarbox, Groton town clerk, who offered to place the eleven-inch silver cup in the display case in the Groton

Town Hall. The well-polished trophy was formally presented, and you can see it there today, resting not far from the site of the oval track where young Christie McConnell won his daring race, traveling a mile a minute.

FISHTOWN

People sometimes ask about Fishtown, an elusive section of Groton never of village status and now largely gone and forgotten. True, we have Fishtown Road, winding south to Noank Road from the junction of Route 1 (New London Road) and Noank Ledyard Road. Years ago we had a Fishtown Chapel, a Fishtown School and a Fishtown Cemetery. The cemetery still exists, although its proper name, under which it was incorporated, is Lower Mystic Cemetery.

It all goes back to the estimable John Fish and his son Samuel. John was said to be "of Mystic" as early as 1655, when he was granted land on the Mystic River north of the Burrows and Packers. John served in the Narragansett War in 1675, but later moved to Stonington. When he died, his estate was divided between his sons, Jonathan and Samuel.

Samuel, born in 1656, was prominent in Groton affairs. He was a captain in the colonial wars, and when Groton gained its independence from New London in 1705, he was elected second townsman. He represented Groton in the General Assembly from 1706 to 1708 and again in 1712. He accumulated

Fishtown School, one of the many one-room schools in Groton of long ago. *Courtesy of Robert Bankel.*

several tracts of land, amounting to about a thousand acres, extending from the Mystic River west to the present Flanders Road, lying on both sides of the present New London Road. In 1695, he built a fine two-story house facing east on what is now Noank Ledyard Road, opposite the extension of Daniel Brown Road. This old house stood well into the twentieth century, but about 1934 it was replaced by a neat modern structure, built on Samuel's original foundations. This later house still stands.

In the early 1800s, as the population increased, a one-room school was built southeast of Samuel's house. Known locally as Fishtown School, it was officially listed as "Flanders School," district 9. The Mystic River Historical Society has a primitive painting of this school, done by a woman who taught there about 1830. In 1900, fourteen pupils attended Fishtown School.

Large families were the rule in those days. You've heard the saying, "There are lots of fish in the sea." There were lots of Fishes in Mystic too, second and third and fourth cousins, all descended from the original John. About 1740, Captain John Fish, who probably earned his title in the militia, built a trim cottage west of the junction of Noank Road and New London Road, a structure that still stands on the north side of the highway. A succession of his descendants later lived in that house.

During the 1890s, a small chapel was built for Sunday school purposes not far from Captain John's house. It stood on the bank, reached by a short flight of stairs. Fishtown Chapel was used for Sunday school and community gatherings. In the 1920s, when the old Fishtown School became too dilapidated, the chapel was used for school sessions. Eventually the old school crumbled into dust; only its foundation remained in the woods. Today, its location has been engulfed by a new housing development.

Appropriately, Fishtown or Lower Mystic Cemetery on New London Road stands on part of Samuel Fish's land. In 1849, when it became unfashionable to bury the dead in small plots on family property, Lower Mystic Cemetery Association was formed. Trustees Jedediah Randall, Silas Beebe, Jeremiah Wilbur and Sanford A.W. Williams purchased one acre and 150 square rods of land from Horatio Nelson Fish Sr. for a burying ground. They paid $294.53, signing the deed on October 1. Horatio and his son, Horatio Jr., are buried there, along with many Mystic sea captains and their wives. The cemetery is now maintained by a board of trustees, which includes descendants of those early families, including a representative of the Fish family.

As times changed, Fishtown Chapel stood forlorn and deserted for years, until Mystic Seaport Museum began to develop the idea of a

Seaport Street on its grounds. In 1949, the museum hired C.P. Maxson to move the building, board by board, from New London Road to the Seaport grounds to become part of the village it was creating. The work was done almost singlehandedly by Giovanni (John) Favretti, the father of Rudy Favretti, retired professor of landscape architecture at the University of Connecticut. Giovanni began the demanding job on June 8, 1949. The chapel was lined with tongue-and-groove beaded woodwork, and he had to be careful not to rip the boards. Also, each board had to be numbered so it could be put together like a giant jigsaw puzzle at its new site.

When the chapel was reconstructed on Seaport Street, the administration decided that it needed a steeple, so Rudy's dad obliged and built one. When he was working, he would ring the bell to tell his wife when he was coming home to Bruggeman Place for his dinner. Fishtown Chapel, a nostalgic part of local history, is happily preserved at the Seaport and is popular for summer weddings.

Fishtown itself is gone now, but it's nice to note that John and Samuel's descendants still own and occupy a part of the original Fish lands in Mystic.

PORTERSVILLE ACADEMY IN 1849

In January 1849, Groton's attention, along with the rest of the country, was directed toward California, where gold had been discovered at Sutter's Mill. All up and down the East Coast men planned how to get there to find treasure for themselves. In Mystic, the schooner *Anthem*, commanded by Captain Thomas Eldredge, had already left. The ship *Trescott* lay in the Mystic River ready to sail, carrying a number of prominent local men. Others in town planned to sail on the *Empire* or on the schooner *Velasco*, which carried members of the "Groton California Company."

A fine send-off program was scheduled in Mystic at the neighborhood schoolhouse, Portersville Academy, for the evening of January 11. The academy stood just north of the Mariners Free Church, near the present location of the Union Baptist Church. Speakers had been well drilled, and the ambitious

Portersville Academy at its original site on Baptist Hill in Mystic, circa 1880. *Courtesy of the Union Baptist Church.*

program included twenty-seven items ranging from dialogues to soliloquies and drama. Audiences in those pre-television days loved long speeches and classical selections. Admission was free, and a huge crowd gathered in the second-floor classroom to enjoy the proceedings. They were seated on makeshift seats, and the room was cheery and warm from the potbellied stove.

Some participants were students at Portersville Academy. Others were talented adult members of the community. A.G. Stark, Mystic River's prominent merchant and builder of the fashionable octagon house, had written two of the numbers. Other items were "Cato's Soliloquy" by Charles Henry Packer, "Song of the Indian Student" by William Fish and a "Specimen of James Otis, 1775," by Giles Wolfe. They were all heavily classical, including "An Original Dialogue on Peace and War," written by William H. Potter, the school principal.

All went well as the program progressed until it was time for the "California Song" sung by Frank Dudley. He entered to great applause, dressed as a miner with spade, sifter and washbowl slung over his shoulder. Just as he began to sing, the south half of the floor began to settle, falling until it was eight feet lower than the other half. When Colonel Amos Clift had built the academy in 1839, he had not planned for as large a crowd as these exercises drew. As the floor fell, the horrified audience began to scream. Rumors spread that dozens of men, women and children were crushed to death beneath the debris.

A great cloud of dust arose from the tan bark between the floors. The worst danger was the stove, full of glowing coals, which fell with the floor. The principal, Mr. Potter, sprang to the rescue. Locating the stove below in the ruins, he directed his pupils to hand snowballs through the windows to put out the fire. He made sure there were no victims crushed on the first floor. In fact, no one was seriously injured, although a few had scratches and bruises and someone was scalded by the basin of hot water that stood on the stove. A collection for repairs was started on the spot. Work began the following day, and according to record, the schoolhouse was ready for use by January 22. They didn't waste time in 1849.

By popular demand, the aborted program was carried out completely on January 19 in the South Conference Room, as the school was not yet ready and both churches had refused to have the program in their quarters. This time the price of admission was twenty-five cents, with Captain George W. Ashby acting as doorkeeper. Proceeds amounted to sixty dollars, apart from subscriptions to repair the school. The program lasted three hours, and the "California Song" was the hit of the show. Sitting in the audience were officers and crew of the ship *Trescott*, including some prominent citizens of the area—Henry D. Chesebro, A. Amesbury, Horace Clift, Hiram Appelman, William H. Denison and others, all set to leave for California. They all joined in the applause.

Portersville Academy later became the property of Groton's Fifth School District. It was used for classes in its location beside the church until 1879, when it was abandoned for school purposes. In 1888, the Town of Groton purchased the two-story building and moved it a block south to the corner of High Street and Old New London Road, where it served as a district hall. When we came to Mystic in 1939, we went there to cast our votes in the November elections. Voting booths were on the first floor, but if you looked up at the ceiling, you could still see patches where the second floor fell through during the "California Song."

The old academy continued to serve area voters until 1958, when it was abandoned by the town. Upstairs, rooms were shuttered and barred, and the empty structure was threatened with demolition. In 1974, the Mystic River Historical Society acquired the academy, then Groton's oldest existing schoolhouse. Under their auspices it has been carefully restored and is a vital part of the society's outreach program, attracting hundreds of schoolchildren each year to participate in the experiences of a nineteenth-century classroom.

FORT HILL SCHOOL

My first teaching job in Groton in 1948 was the first grade at Fort Hill School in Poquonnock Bridge, located in the federal housing project called Fort Hill Homes. This sprawling complex of 1,110 units of single and double houses was built in 1942 to house government employees and defense workers. World War II ended in 1945, but three years later the homes were still fully occupied by a transient population. People were finishing enlistment and moving away, while others came to take their places. Some houses still stand at the foot of Fort Hill, but the buildings housing the school are long gone.

The original houses were laid out south of Route 1 around Midway Oval. On Central Avenue, the government had provided a modest four-room, cinder-block school. With the ensuing baby boom, it was far from adequate. Each year classes overflowed into the large wooden community house that stood across the street, its playground equipped with slides, monkey bars and swings.

In 1949, the school had already taken over the nursery school quarters and a large classroom at the eastern end of the building. I was scheduled to use the poolroom. Late in August they took out the pool table and put in tables, chairs and a portable blackboard, squeezed a teacher's desk in the corner and presto, a first-grade classroom!

There still was not enough space to keep up with the tremendous population explosion. Groton's population increased 100.7 percent between 1940 and 1950, and existing buildings housed the influx of new pupils with double sessions and overcrowded classrooms. While the town feverishly raced to build new schools, many classrooms saw double use every day. My first graders came at 8:00 a.m. and left at 12:00 p.m. Another teacher taught a different class in the room from 12:30 p.m. to 4:30 p.m. My crew was half asleep when they arrived, and the later group faced winter darkness when they left.

We didn't have desks for the kids, just small tables, each accommodating two. We were pretty crowded in that room with thirty-four first graders. The fire marshal would disapprove these days because it was hard to get in and out of the seats. There was no place for storage. Each child kept notebooks, pencils, crayons and small necessities in a large, labeled manila envelope. When the session ended, we collected them and kept them overnight in the closet that formerly housed pool cues. Textbooks were stored in a bookcase and passed out at every session, and there was little space to display art or any of the work done by the children.

The school principal was Mrs. Edith Tyler, a human dynamo. She wore impossibly high heels and traveled at lightning speed all day. She reigned supreme in the little, white, cinder-block school, her iron rule extending strongly across the street into the community house. She never let us forget who was in charge. But she was a wonderful administrator, a necessary talent in such a complex situation, and she was also great with the kids. But teachers and pupils alike trembled when we heard the *tap-tap* of those high heels.

Fort Hill School was a pleasant place to teach. It was uncomplicated. Everyone walked to school. There was no hot lunch program; everyone went home for lunch. Everything was gloriously middle class. There were no first families in this new housing project; everyone had arrived at approximately the same time, and in the postwar economy there was no great wealth. Everyone was comfortable in this community. There was no keeping up with the Joneses.

However, double sessions were hard on teachers and pupils alike. The day was rushed and we missed fun things that normally go with first grade. We had no library. Every week I checked out twenty different children's books from the Mystic and Noank Library and carted them to Fort Hill School for my first graders to enjoy. I loved teaching beginning reading. But we used the reading series known universally as "Dick and Jane," which was far from inspirational. It was a transient population with pupils coming and going throughout the year. We coined a little motto—"Teach them to read and they move to California." Then we would have to take their replacements through Dick and Jane all over again.

Groton eventually built new schools in the Poquonnock area. First came Poquonnock Bridge School, now part of Fitch Middle School. Then came Claude Chester School, which still exists. I don't know what happened to the original cinder-block Fort Hill School; it was probably torn down. But the wooden community house burned some years later, when it housed the offices of the Groton Public Schools.

GROTON'S THREE LIBRARIES

Groton people must love books. There are three libraries in the town, all busily supplying the needs of the populace. The oldest, Bill Memorial

The Mystic and Noank Library, a gift of Captain Elihu Spicer, opened in 1894.

The Groton Public Library, established in 1960, moved into its present quarters in 1977. *Courtesy of the Groton Public Library.*

on Groton Heights, dates to 1888, when philanthropist Frederic Bill purchased seventeen hundred books to establish the town's first library in honor of his sisters, Eliza and Harriet. Perhaps he was influenced by his brother Henry, who had created a library in Ledyard as early as 1867.

Before the Civil War, Frederic worked in his family's publishing business, but later he organized a firm in New York City that specialized in linen manufacture. This was so successful that he retired to a fine mansion on the banks of the Thames when he was only forty.

The first books were kept in the district schoolhouse until Bill donated a fine building to house the collection. The library, dedicated on June 18, 1890, was designed by Stephen C. Earle and constructed of Stony Creek granite trimmed with Maynard freestone. It also boasted a red slate roof. Additions made in 1907 were in the same attractive architectural style and provided space for a natural history museum.

On the opposite side of town, another philanthropist acted. Captain Elihu Spicer, born in Noank in 1825, had sailed vessels for Charles Mallory of Mystic and later acted as partner in the Mallory firm, amassing a nice fortune. He decided to build a library for the residents of Mystic and Noank, choosing a spot on Elm Street in Mystic just opposite his lavish summer home. Plans were drawn up by architects William Higginson and William Bigelow for the two-story building constructed of granite from Leete's Island and red sandstone from Longmeadow, Massachusetts, with green tile roofing. The original building was enlarged for its centennial in 1994.

The library, containing four thousand books, was dedicated on January 23, 1894. Unfortunately, Captain Spicer did not live to see his gift complete. He was thrown from his carriage when his frisky mustang bolted in November 1892. He died two months later as a result of his injuries. The Bill Memorial and the Mystic and Noank Library are endowed institutions, governed by their own trustees and privately financed. In 1957, the Mystic and Noank Library received a token grant from the town to enable it to increase its services, but both remain more or less neighborhood resources, not intended to serve the entire town. Groton did not have a town library, one that was entirely tax supported, until the Groton Public Library opened on July 5, 1960, in the small brick building on Route 1 that had once been Poquonnock Bridge School. (This is now the social services headquarters at 2 Fort Hill Road.)

The Groton Public Library was an idea whose time had come. The little building was extensively used under the direction of Martha

Hagerty, the first librarian. It was soon apparent that a new and larger building was needed to support the increase in circulation and the growing size of the collections.

Under the direction of librarian Gretchen Hammerstein, the attractive new modern building was planned and erected on Route 117, Newtown Road, the former site of the Ackley turkey farm. Books were moved to the new building in August 1977 with the help of the 162nd Battalion, Connecticut National Guard, and a host of loyal volunteers and staff. The library was opened officially on December 15, 1977.

This building also needed an addition, as through the years its services to the town continued to grow. Attesting to its success, the Groton Public Library and Information Center received the 2005 Connecticut Award for Excellence in Public Library Services.

Groton's three outstanding libraries provide books and wonderful information to the town's residents. With three libraries within its borders, Groton is a lucky town.

Written for the Groton Tercentennial Committee.

ABOUT THE AUTHOR

Carol W. Kimball had to bone up on Groton history to teach her third-grade social studies classes. She found it so interesting that it became a hobby. She was appointed Groton municipal historian in 1985. Her articles have appeared in many periodicals, including *Yankee Magazine* and the *Log of Mystic Seaport*. She has authored several books, including *The Groton Story*, *The Poquonnock Bridge Story* and *Historic Glimpses*, and since 1985, she has written a weekly column about local history for *The Day*, a New London, Connecticut newspaper.